# Build 25 Beautiful
# BOXES

Doug Stowe

POPULAR WOODWORKING BOOKS

CINCINNATI, OHIO
popularwoodworking.com

# Build 25 Beautiful
# BOXES

Doug Stowe

# CONTENTS

# ABOUT THE AUTHOR

Doug Stowe began his career as a woodworker in 1976, making custom furniture and small boxes. He has written how-to articles for a variety of woodworking magazines and is the author of numerous box-making books. His book "Making Elegant Custom Tables" won the 2003 Golden Hammer Award for the best how-to book. His boxes and furniture have been featured in *Woodworkers Journal, Woodwork, American Woodworker, Wood Magazine* and *Fine Woodworking*.

He is the founder of the woodworking program Wisdom of the Hands at the Clear Spring School in Eureka Springs, Arizona. The program integrates woodworking activities to stimulate and reinforce academic curricula, restoring the rationale for the use of crafts in general education. In 2009 he was named an "Arkansas Living Treasure" by the Arkansas Department of Heritage and Arkansas Arts Council for his contributions to traditional crafts and craft education. He maintains a strong advocacy for hands-on learning through his blog, Wisdom of the Hands: wisdomofhands.blogspot.com

# FOREWORD

In 1996, I was contacted by David Lewis, acquisitions editor at F+W asking whether I would be interested in writing a book about boxes. At the time, I had published a couple articles in woodworking magazines and had been inspired by the books and philosophy of James Krenov, whom I sought to emulate in my work.

David had visited a small shop in my hometown of Eureka Springs and had discovered my small inlaid boxes for sale in a shop. Upon returning home to Cincinnati, he called to ask whether I'd be interested in writing a book. I wanted to write a "why-to book," like Krenov's not a "how-to book." David and I found a compromise that combined projects with "why-to" sidebars that allowed me to share my own philosophy of woodworking in a context that empowered others to make beautiful boxes in their own shops.

That conversation led to two best selling books, "Creating Beautiful Boxes with Inlay Techniques," and "Simply Beautiful Boxes." In the process of writing those first two books, I was transformed. I learned there is no better way to share philosophical ideas than through the shared making of beautiful and useful things. Starting out as a small town woodworker, I was given the opportunity to write for and teach a larger audience – there is no better subject in the field of woodworking than making a wooden box.

You may invest just as much skill in a wooden box as in any larger project, and you can learn just as much. The materials are inexpensive, or can be derived from scrap. Boxes are perfectly suited to working in small spaces, too. So, in that light, boxes make ideal projects for beginning woodworkers.

25 of the box projects from those two books have now been compiled and are presented in this volume along with an appendix based on my original "why-to" sidebars (see page 181). As you choose projects from this book, keep in mind that the many of the boxes build upon the techniques learned from one another, and that vary in complexity and difficulty. So it's a good idea to study the entire book before undertaking any particular project.

*An important note about safety:* Making boxes can involve working with small workpieces and making intricate cuts. Some of the photos in this book show machinery turned off and with guards removed as to show the intricacies of the cut. It is important to use every precaution when planning your cuts. Wherever possible use push blocks and other safety devices to minimize risk (especially if it is necessary to remove a machine's guard in order to make a cut). See Appendix B on page 189 for additional notes on safety and a pattern for my favorite push stick design.

I want to thank the editors of Popular Woodworking Books for helping me to keep these projects alive and available to readers and box makers of all ages. I also want to thank an earlier generation of editors and staff at F+W for encouraging me to write and share my ideas.

—*Doug Stowe*

# THE ART OF INLAY

Before diving into the box projects in this book, it's a good idea to take a look at inlay techniques. While you can purchase commercial inlays, nothing enhances a box and adds a personal touch better than inlay that you've created yourself. Inlay is perceived to be a more advanced woodworking technique requiring a great deal of patience and skill. For this reason, many woodworkers are reluctant to try it. However, it is easy to create your own inlays and use them to enhance your woodworking projects. Making inlay, for me, is a form of workshop play; an opportunity to experiment and see what I can come up with. The woods themselves, the colors, the patterns of grain, their various levels of reflectivity of light and their smells as they pass through the saw are a source of enjoyment for me. For some woodworkers, doing inlay work is a way they can demonstrate their woodworking expertise. Personally, I like to use my craftsmanship to give voice to the natural characteristics of the wood and use the inlay techniques to focus attention on the wood's beauty rather than on my skill as a craftsman.

# MAKING CHECKERBOARD INLAY

## Preparing the Stock
Start by cutting ½" x 1¼" blocks of crotch walnut and fiddleback maple from ¾" x 1¼" stock. Use the sliding cutoff table on the table saw, and a stop-block to maintain uniformity.

## Arrange and Glue the First Pattern
After the pieces are cut, arrange them in an alternating pattern – walnut, maple, walnut – fanning a long sting of patterned blocks. After you have organized the pattern, apply glue to all surfaces that contact other surfaces and then use a bar clamp to pull them tight, as shown in making the inlay for the simple inlaid box in chapter one. To keep them flat and straight, glue them up on a flat board, removing them from the board when the clamp is tight. Sight down the glued-up stock to ensure that the row of blocks is still straight, and shim the row out away from the bar or clamp it toward the bar, if necessary.

## Rip ½" Strips From the Inlay Pattern
After the glue has had plenty of time to set, joint two edges flat and square on the jointer, set up the table saw with a thin-kerf crosscut blade and rip the strip into two ½"-wide strips. These two strips will be glued back together, offset to form the ½" squares.

## Glue-Up the New Pattern
Use two ⅛"-thick walnut strips as border stock, and spread glue on each surface to be glued. Use long strips of wood to cushion and distribute the pressure from the bar clamps, and use about six clamps to glue a 30" section.

## Cut the Inlay
After this block has been glued for several hours, unclamp it and joint one face on the jointer. Then set up the table saw with a thin-kerf ripping blade and saw the inlay block into thin strips (³⁄₃₂" to ⅛" thick). Use a zero-clearance insert in the table saw to reduce risk of the inlay coming apart or jumping around while ripping the strips. The finished inlay is 1¼" wide, and you get about five strips from the gluing-and-cutting procedure.

Use the cutoff box on the table saw and a stop-block to make sure all the pieces are the same size. The cutoff box is a simple jig that rides in the grooves in the table saw top allowing accurate cutting of parts.

After arranging the blocks in the alternating pattern, apply glue to the end grain on both ends before placing pieces back in the arrangement.

# MAKING THE TRIANGLE INLAY

## Cut Angled Pieces
To make the triangle-pattern inlay, use the cutoff box on the table saw with a fence made of a piece of plywood tacked on the surface of the table with brads. The exact angle used for this is not critical: Turning the stock over between cuts will give each piece the same angle on each side to ensure fitting with neighboring pieces. I used sassafras, pecan and honey locust to cut the triangles for this inlay.

Use the cutoff box and angled guide with a stop-block to cut uniform triangles for the patterned inlay.

After arranging the pieces in the pattern, spread glue on all sides of each triangle and the walnut border strips. Use bar clamps and hardwood blocking to clamp the parts together, forming a block of inlay that will yield several inlay strips.

## Assemble the Pattern

To assemble this pattern, spread glue on each piece alternating the species of wood in a pecan-honey locust-sassafras-pecan pattern. After spreading glue on the ⅛" walnut border strips, clamp the parts together using bar clamps and hardwood blocks to keep the inlay block straight.

## OTHER VARIETIES

The number of patterns you can make is infinite. By gluing simple strips of wood together and cutting the glued-up block into angled slices, I make another simple but pleasing design. To glue up a pattern like this requires extra care to keep the parts in alignment, so clamp side blocks in place to keep parts from shifting while the bar clamp pulls the pieces tightly together.

## NOW, DESIGN YOUR OWN

I invite you to use these simple processes as your own jumping-off point into this form of workshop play and experimentation. You will come up many ideas of your own.

With the cutoff box, cut thin slices from a block formed of various hardwoods.

With the slices alternating, glue them back together into a patterned block. When resawn on the band saw, the block will yield several inlay strips.

# SLIDING CUTOFF TABLE

The sliding cutoff table is a simple device that I use to accurately cut parts to uniform length. For example, when cutting the front and back of a box, the most important thing is not the exact length in terms of inches, but that both parts be exactly the same length. By using a stop-block clamped to the fence of the cutoff table and by pushing the workpiece against the stop-block, each piece cut will be exactly the same. This is important whether cutting parts for a single box or 20, because when working on the small scale that boxes present, even 1/64" is noticeable in the opening and closing of a lid. I frequently use a cutoff table without the fence when cutting very small and irregularly shaped parts. If you have ever tried to hold something really small safely using a standard miter gauge, you know the difficulties involved. As shown in some of the projects of the book, I use small brads to secure fences made of 1/4" plywood at a variety of angles as needed, to make various small parts, and small stop-blocks secured with brads to help hold the parts in the exact position needed. In this way, I can use very simple and direct methods for making accurately dimensioned small and angled parts. A word of caution: You must remember that the blade, that is making a through cut will appear on the other side of the fence, unguarded. I am very careful to keep my hands and other items, such as already cut parts, out of the line of cut. It's easy to construct a cutoff table with a simple guard at the back side, and I recommend it.

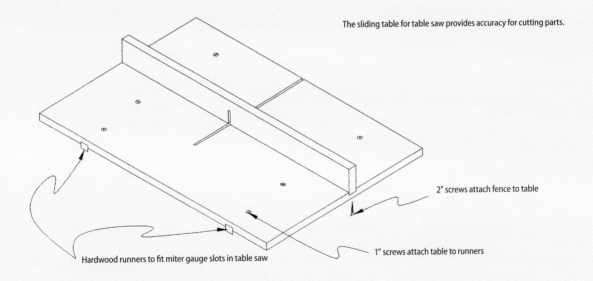

The sliding table for table saw provides accuracy for cutting parts.

2" screws attach fence to table

1" screws attach table to runners

Hardwood runners to fit miter gauge slots in table saw

# CHAPTER ONE

# SIMPLE INLAID BOX

A simple inlaid box was one of my first commercial products. Designed for a jeweler in my hometown to use as presentation boxes to be sold with his jewelry, I made them in a variety of shapes and sizes for rings, necklaces and bracelets. His customers became interested in them and asked to purchase them without jewelry. I suddenly found myself in the box business and made hundreds in this design over a period of several years. I found box-making to be a great supplement to my woodworking business, keeping me busy between furniture commissions.

This box body is made without mechanical fasteners and relies only on the glued joint holding the ends to the top and sides, which are cut from a single piece of wood. This is not the ideal way to join wood (given its tendency to expand and contract) and one would certainly have greater difficulties with this design if it were made larger. Perhaps it was beginner's luck that has held so many of them together for 20 years, but I have several of them around that still show no sign of coming apart. I often come across them on the coffee tables of old friends. I present this technique because it was the start of my own box-building adventure.

My first step in making this box was to edge join ⅞" walnut stock long enough to make the tops and bottoms of the planned boxes, then rip it about 1/16" oversize and pass it through the planer at 3" to attain the desired width. To make a box with a 7" inside length (long enough to hold pens, but not pencils), I used a piece of walnut 14½" long.

## MATERIALS LIST

| Brass hinges | 1 pr. | 1" x ¹³⁄₁₆" open |
|---|---|---|
| Top and bottom | 2 pcs. | ⅞" x 3" x 6¾" |
| Ends | 4 pcs. | ⁵⁄₁₆" x ¹⁵⁄₁₆" x 3⅛" |
| 4/4 Cherry, sassafras, ash, walnut and maple | | 3" x 6" |
| Stips of walnut | 2 pcs. | ⅛" x 1" *(for inlay borders)* |

## TOOLS LIST

Table saw
Jointer
Planer
Bar clamps
Belt or disc sander
Router table
1" straight-cut router bit

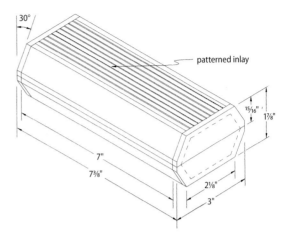

## MAKING THE PATTERNED INLAY

I began making this type of inlay a very short time after I began my woodworking career. I have continued to refine and use this technique for 20 years because it is a simple way to share my interest in the variety of North American hardwoods and help people to better understand the wealth of our forests. I start with 1"-thick pieces of wood from several species. Some of my favorites to use for inlay are walnut, cherry, elm, sassafras, maple, persimmon, honey locust and ash. I like to use woods that contrast in texture and grain as well as color, and while these woods could be cut in to much smaller pieces (making the inlay much more intricate), it is important to me to allow enough of the natural characteristics of each wood to remain. Someone should be able to look at a piece and say, "So, that's what sassafras looks like."

### Cut Stock Into 1" Strips

Taking the 1"-thick pieces of various hardwoods, join one side flat and one edge straight and square, and then rip the pieces to a uniform width, about twice the width of the planned inlay, on the table saw.

### Cut to Length

Next, cut the pieces into lengths about ⅝" long, using a cutoff box on the table saw.

### Glue-Up Strips

Next, arrange the pieces of the various woods in a pattern, with the pieces lined up end grain to end grain. After you have arranged your pattern, apply glue to each piece. Because you are gluing end grain, apply plenty of glue to both parts. As they are glued, place them back in the arranged order. In order to work with a safe cutting length on the table saw, I usually glue up lengths from about 18" to 36", arranging them along a piece of scrap wood ½" shorter than the length of the pieces. After glue is applied to all the pieces except the end pieces, use a bar clamp to pull the pieces tight. At this point always be careful to make sure that all of the pieces have stayed in place. They tend to move around a bit as the clamp applies pressure, so chase them back in place. When you are

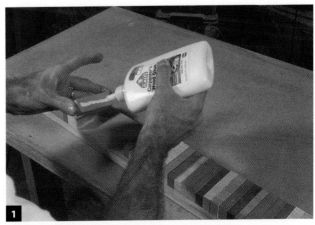

**1** Apply plenty of glue when joining end grain. Lay the pattern out dry first and follow the same arrangement as the glue is applied.

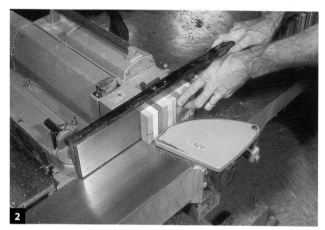

**2**

After the glue is dry, joint one edge 90° to the face.

satisfied that the pieces are being glued up where you want them, lift the clamped and glued pieces off the piece of scrap wood and set them aside to dry. If the glued-up block shows any sign of bending toward or away from the bar clamp, insert shims between the block and the bar (or use a C-clamp to pull the block closer to the bar). Being certain the glued-up inlay block is flat will ensure that you are able to get the maximum number of inlay strips from the block. After the glue is dry, remove the clamp. Joint one face and one edge flat on the jointer.

## Rip the Inlay Into Thin Strips

Using a sharp thin-kerf carbide blade in the table saw, begin ripping thin strips from the glued-up hardwood block. I usually rip the first strips thicker, and work my way down to the thinner strips. Ripping thin strips on the table saw is a delicate and dangerous operation that calls for the use of push blocks and requires a zero-clearance table saw blade insert to give the strips firm support and keep them from chattering and bouncing. Rather than risk injury, always plan the glued-up block to be wide enough to allow for some waste.

## Make the Inlay Border

Next, rip walnut into thin strips, about ⅛" x 1", that will be used as the border strips to surround the pattern.

**3**

Begin ripping thin strips from the block you created by gluing up the hardwood pieces. Make sure you put the flat face on the table and your 90° edge on the fence.

**4**

Rearrange the strips into a visually pleasing pattern and glue them together. The trick here is to maintain symmetry and smooth movement within the pattern.

**5**

Use blocks of hard wood on both sides of the strip when you clamp it to ensure both good distribution of clamping pressure and that the finished strips come out straight.

## Arrange the Inlay Pattern

After the strips are cut from the patterned block, rearrange them in relation to each other, sliding them into a visually pleasing pattern. When you have the pattern you want, mark across it with a pencil. As the slices are glued this will help you know how to place them back in the desired relationship. Apply glue to one of the walnut border strips, then to each strip in succession. Finish with the other border strip. Be careful to make sure that each strip is laid in its exact position before you lay the next one. In a wide pattern, the bottom strips will start to get a good glue grip by the time the second border strip goes on. Use blocks of hardwood on both sides of the strip when clamping. This ensures good distribution of clamping pressure and helps the strips to come out straight. I usually use several bar clamps along the length of the strip and apply a lot of pressure to make sure the strips get a good grip on each other. By this time, I'm usually ready to let the patterned blocks sit overnight before releasing the clamps.

## Rip the Pattern Strips

After releasing the clamps, join the face flat and begin ripping thin patterned strips on the table saw. Use the thin-kerf blade, the zero-clearance insert and a push stick for safety when ripping thin strips. The very last strip takes special care because it is so thin and so close to the saw blade. Use a push block for this final cut to keep your hands safe.

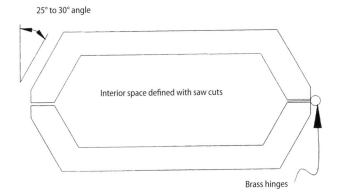

25° to 30° angle

Interior space defined with saw cuts

Brass hinges

## INLAYING THE TOP

Inlay the top before the shape is cut in the box because it is easiest to clamp the inlay in place during gluing while the top is still a squared block of solid wood. Mounting a 1" straight-cut router bit in the router table, set the height of cut to just less than the thickness of your finished inlay strips. Set the fence on the router table to cut 1"-wide channels where you want the inlay strips to fit. The finished inlay strip I made for this use is about 1½" wide before joining and sizing, so I cut the channel wider with a second pass. This widens the distance between the bit and the fence to its finished width of 1⅜". Make the first cut moving the workpiece along the fence and widen the channel by adjusting the fence and moving the workpiece in the opposite direction to make the second cut. This technique avoids a climb-cut, which can grab the workpiece and pull fingers into the moving bit in the router table.

**6**

Using the router table, inlay the top before the shape is cut. Set the height of cut to just less than the thickness of the finished inlay strips. This will give you room to sand the installed inlay flush with the top. Set the fence on the router table to cut 1"-channels the width of the inlay strips.

Make the first cut moving the workpiece along the fence, and the second cut to widen the channel by adjusting the fence and moving the workpiece in the opposite direction.

The final fitting is done on the router table. To avoid the danger of climb-feeding on the router table, pass the inlay pieces from left to right between the fence and the router bit.

A guard placed over the router bit helps to make this a safe cut.

Spread glue evenly inside the channel to prevent squeezout on the top of the box.

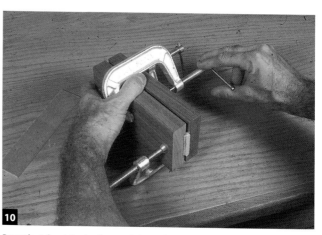

Press the inlay strips in place and clamp them with a backing strip thick enough to evenly distribute the clamping pressure.

## Size the Inlay

After the channel is cut to about ⅛" narrower than the inlay strip, size the strips by first cutting them the length of the wood to be inlaid, and then passing one edge across the jointer to make it flat. Try to take enough off with the jointer so that, when the strip is finish-fitted, the border around the pattern will be approximately even on both sides. The final fitting is done on the router table. Raise the 1" cutter up above the thickness of the inlay and set the width between the cutter and the fence equal to the width of the channel. Follow a trial-and-error procedure in this: Using a test strip made from scrap, cut the strip a bit wide at first and move the fence in closer to get a good fit. When the scrap piece fits snug, with no spaces on either side, and

is not too difficult to set in place, cut the inlay strips to size.

## Trim and Install the Inlay

To avoid the danger of climb-feeding on the router table, pass the inlay pieces from left to right between the fence and the router bit, against the direction of the cutter. Use a push stick to keep your fingers safe, and place a guard over the router bit for additional safety. Apply glue to the inside of the routed channel, spread it evenly with your fingers, and then press the inlay strips in place and clamp them with a backing strip thick enough to evenly distribute the clamping pressure. Use C-clamps for this job.

The first cut on the inside of the box should be right in the middle.

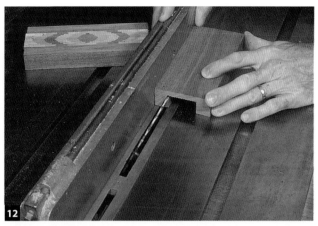

With the angle of the blade at 35°, cut away the final sections to form the hollow of the box.

Raise the blade height to just over the full thickness of the workpiece and reset the fence to shape the outside of the box.

Assemble the boxes by applying glue to the ends of the box bodies and then placing the end pieces in position. Use a flat scrap board to build a row of the tops and bottoms together, and then use a bar clamp and end blocks to pull the joints tight.

# FORMING THE INSIDE OF THE BOX

## Make 90° Cuts on the Table Saw

Form the inside of the box by making repetitive saw cuts, the kerf of each cut adding to the space within the box. Use a blade that leaves a V-shaped crown. Be careful to adjust the fence for each cut so the repeating kerfs form a delicate pattern on the bottom surface of the inside of the box. Many of my customers comment positively about this unique feature, which would be lost if care was not taken in setting up the fence and the surface became rough and unattractive. Make the initial cuts with the blade set at 90° on the table saw, positioning the first cut at the exact center, moving the fence away from the blade just less than the width of the kerf, turning the workpiece end over end to cut on both sides, and making these cuts until the opening is 1¾" wide.

## Make the Angle Cuts

Change the angle of the blade to about 30° from perpendicular, and raise it so that it cuts at the same height as the cuts made at 90°. Adjust the fence so that the blade cuts the final section away to form the hollow of the box.

Cut the corners off the end pieces with the table saw, with the blade still tilted at the same angle as for defining the outside shape.

Use a belt sander to sand the box ends even with the tops and bottoms.

## Cut Off the Sides

With the blade set at the same angle, raise the blade height to just over the full thickness of the workpiece and set the fence to cut the matching angle on the outside of the box.

## ASSEMBLING THE BOX

Now that the interior shape of the box is defined, the next job is to cut the shaped box bodies to length and glue on the end pieces. The ends, made of walnut, are from stock resawn on the table saw and planed to dimension. Each box requires four end pieces, which are made oversize in length and width to allow for inaccuracies in clamping and gluing the pieces in place.

### Cut the Parts to Size

Using the cutoff box on the table saw, cut the box bodies to length desired, and then cut the end pieces to the finished length.

### Attach the End Pieces

Assemble the boxes by applying glue to the ends of the box bodies and then placing the end pieces in position. Use a flat scrap board to build a row of the tops and bottoms together, and then use a bar clamp and end blocks to pull the joints tight. Immediately and carefully check to see that each end is in acceptable position, and quickly loosen the clamps to reposition the end pieces if there has been any squirming. Because using only one bar clamp could allow the boxes to jump out of the clamping arrangement, set the boxes down on the floor or table top with the clamp up. Leave the clamp in place for several hours to make sure the glue has an opportunity to set firmly.

## FINAL SHAPING & SANDING

### Trim the End Pieces

Cut the corners off the end pieces with the table saw, with the blade still tilted at the same angle as for defining the outside shape. Move the fence over just a little to allow for some of the end pieces to be sanded off.

### Rough Sand the Sides

Use the stationary belt sander to sand the box ends even with the tops and bottoms. Sand the tops, bottoms, angles, sides and the flat areas where the tops and bottoms will come together, starting out with #100-grit and moving to #150-grit.

## INSTALLING THE HINGES

### Cut the Hinge Mortises

Once the rough sanding is complete, and prior to orbital sanding, cut the mortises for the 1"-wide hinges to fit. Do this on the router table by setting up a stop block on the table to control the movement of the box over the 1" router bit. Set the height of the router bit at just under half the thickness of the hinge. After cutting one mortise in the top and bottom, relocate the stop block to rout the matching mortises.

## Predrill Screw Holes for the Hinges

Use a jig to make sure the holes for the hinges are placed properly, and predrill for the hinges with a ¹⁄₁₆" drill bit. Use a bit of beeswax on the threads of the screws to lubricate them so they don't break off in the hole. Before the final sanding, sand the ends and front edge of the assembled box on the belt sander to make sure they are in perfect alignment. Then do the finish sanding with a random orbit sander, going #180-grit to #240-grit, and finishing with #320.

## FINISHING

I originally used Deft semi-gloss Clear Wood Finish to finish these boxes, polishing them smooth with 0000 steel wool between the two coats, and again when the finish was dry to soften the gloss enough to hide any irregularities in the brushed-on surface. Now I use Deft Danish Oil, which I prefer because it is a wipe-on, wipe-off finish that does not smell as bad as the lacquer-based Deft. I am careful to keep the shop well-ventilated during my finishing operations. I spread the used rags out outdoors to fully dry before disposing of them.

**17**

Using the router table, cut the spaces for the hinges to fit.

# CHAPTER TWO

# KOA BOX

This box is made from a piece of koa brought to me by my Hawaiian cousins. Made with a simple band saw technique, a block of wood is cut apart into components and then glued back together, leaving out the parts that had formed the interior space. This is a very popular technique and simple enough for a beginner to have success building his or her skills in the use of the band saw or scrollsaw. Many woodworkers have used these basic techniques to develop creative and artistic work. Making a box like this is fun, and gives you a chance to play. I decided to make two, cutting them apart after defining the interior compartments.

## MATERIALS LIST

| | | |
|---|---|---|
| Hawaiian koa | 1 pc. | 1 b.f. x 1⅛" |
| Strips of pecan, sassafras and honey locust | | ¾" x 1" |
| Strips of walnut | | ⅛" x ¾" *(for inlay)* |

## TOOLS LIST

Scrollsaw

Band saw

Router

Router table

Table saw

Belt sander

Orbital sander

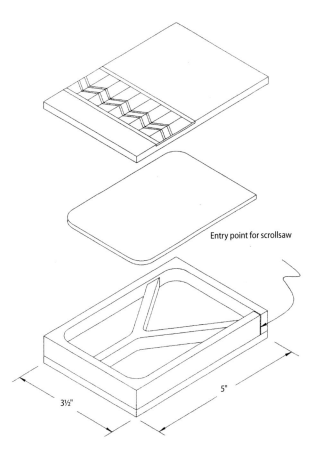

Entry point for scrollsaw

5"

3½"

Use found objects to lay out the design. Here I use a washer to give shape to a corner.

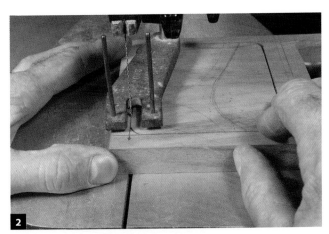

On the scrollsaw, follow the cut line to define the interior of the box.

## SHAPING THE BOX

### Cut Away the Top and Bottom

Begin this box by cutting away the bottom and top from the block of koa using the band saw. Carefully check the tracking of the band saw blade before you start so that you are able to cut uniform ¼"-thick slices from the top and bottom. Next, resurface all the pieces to remove the band saw marks and to provide a good gluing surface when the pieces go back together.

### Cut Out the Interior

Draw the desired interior shape onto the block using found objects to define the space from the center of the original block. I used a can and a washer for this one. Scrollsaw carefully into one corner from the outside and then saw around the perimeter, forming the inside of the box. A band saw can also be used for this.

**3**

Cut away a thin slice of the waste pieces to use as the parts of the lids that locate their positions on the boxes.

**4**

Return to your found objects to mark the center waste pieces for cutting out the dividers.

## Remove the Lid Keeper and Interior Dividers

Set up the ripping fence on the band saw, setting the fence about 3/16" from the blade so that you can surface the lid keeper to about 1/8" before gluing it to the lid. Cut the divider for the inside of the box from the remaining piece. Use the found objects again to mark the interior dividers and cut out the divider parts with the scrollsaw. Hand sand the inside of the box and the divider, using a small rasp to clean up some of the tight spots. Sandpaper can be used with a flat stick for the convex areas, and wrapped on a dowel for some of the concave parts of the divider. Because the box will be lined with flocking, don't worry about achieving a perfect finish. The flocking will cover the sanding marks.

## ASSEMBLING THE BOX

### Mark and Glue the Lid Keepers

Trace the position of the lid keepers with a pencil, marking their location for gluing to the inside of the lid. Then spread glue on the parts and clamp them in the position indicated by the pencil lines. Spread glue on the box body where it intersects the bottom. Use a business card to work a little glue into the saw-kerf left when the inside piece was cut away. Fill the saw-kerf with a thin sliver of wood and use a bar clamp to squeeze this joint closed, and then clamp the bottom in place with several C-clamps. Because you will use a flocked lining, don't worry too much if a little glue squeezes out; it can easily be cleaned away with a small chisel when it is slightly dry but still rubbery.

## MAKING THE INLAY

Inlay this box after it is fully assembled. Making the inlay used in this box is described in this book's introduction, "The Art of Inlay."

## FLOCKING THE INTERIOR

I use Donjer flocking to line the inside of the box. To use this product, brush on the colored adhesive and then either spray on the rayon flocking material with the flocking sprayer or simply put a few tablespoons of flocking material in the box, close the lid and shake.

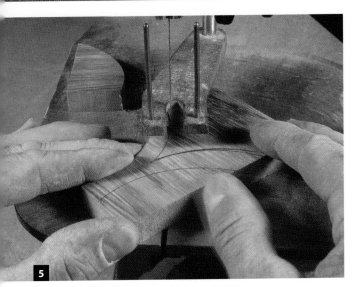

**5**

Cut out the shape of the dividers with the scrollsaw.

**6**

Use a pencil to trace the inside shape of the box on the lid to accurately position the inside parts of the lid.

**7**

Spread glue on the inside lid parts and clamp them to the lid stock. You can see how the lid keeper locks the lid in place.

**8**

Spread glue on the midsections of the box and then clamp them to the box bottom.

# CHAPTER THREE

# PEN BOX

Making the pen box is a very simple exercise in box building and is a good skill builder. The commercial inlays are easy to use, and while it is my feeling that they do not have as much character or personal interest as those I make in my shop, they can enhance the beauty of simple projects quite well. Offsetting the location of the inlay toward the front edge of the lid gives the user an indication of which side to open and is more visually stimulating than having the inlay centered in the box top. This box can be easily modified to meet a number of uses, but I would hesitate to make it very large because of the stresses involved in the expansion and contraction of wood.

## MATERIALS LIST

| Cherry | | $^3/_{16}$" x 3½" x 24" |
|---|---|---|
| Top and bottom | 2 pcs. | 2¾" x 2" x 6" |
| Ends | 2 pcs. | 2¾" x 1¾" 1¼" |
| 5mm barrel hinges | 4 pcs. | |
| Commercial inlay | | |

*This yields enough stock for two boxes.*

## TOOLS LIST

| Table saw |
|---|
| $^1/_{16}$" roundover bit |
| Chamfering bit |
| 5mm brad-point bit |
| Drill press |
| Router table with straight-cut bits |
| Bar clamp |

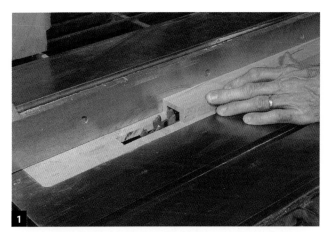

Cut the inside shape of the pen box with a dado blade, cutting the top and bottom of the cherry box in a single operation and moving the fence to widen the cut.

With a straight-cut router bit set to just less than the thickness of the commercial inlay strip, rout the channel for the inlay.

# MAKING THE PEN BOX

## Form the Box Interior

Form the interior shape of the box on the table saw. Set the height of the cut to leave about $^3/_{16}$" of material at the bottom of the box, and cut the entire length at the same time. Because you want the top of the box to be smaller in proportion to the bottom, plane down the top, removing material from the open side of the box.

## Cut the Box to Length

Cut the box parts using the cutoff box on the table saw.

## Drill Holes for the Barrel Hinges

Drill to fit the miniature barrel hinges after carefully drilling a test piece and checking the depth with a dial caliper. To set up for drilling perfectly matched holes, left and right, first drill the holes on one side of all the parts, using a stop-block clamped onto the fence on the drill press. Then drill through a piece of scrap wood and turn that over, using it to set the stop on the fence to position the other holes. This yields left and right holes that match perfectly. To compensate for the differing thickness of the top and bottom, use a shim piece rather than change the depth of the

drilling to adjust the height. You can see this operation in detail in chapter nine.

## Inlay the Top

To inlay the top, select a straight-cut router bit equal to the width of the inlay strip. Raise the cutter height to just barely less than the thickness of the strip. Set the fence to position the strip off-center to indicate which side opens. Then rout the channel for the inlay strip. The commercial inlay is sized to slip right in place. Spread a little glue in the channel. Use a strip of wood cut just a little narrower than the inlay strip as a block to distribute clamping pressure.

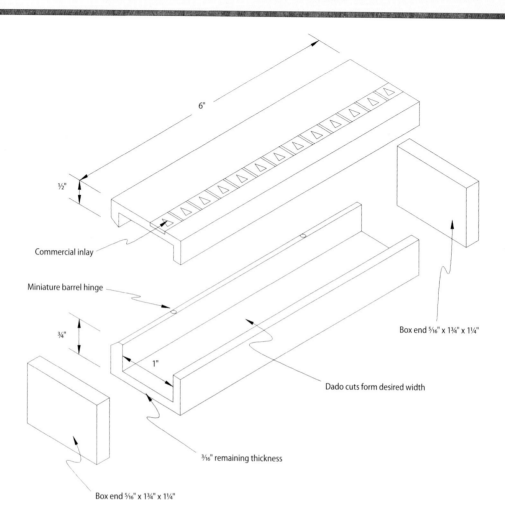

6"

½"

Commercial inlay

Miniature barrel hinge

¾"

1"

Box end ⁵⁄₁₆" x 1¾" x 1¼"

Dado cuts form desired width

³⁄₁₆" remaining thickness

Box end ⁵⁄₁₆" x 1¾" x 1¼"

**3**

Use a 45° chamfering bit in the router to provide clearance to operate the hinges.

## Chamfer the Edges

Rout a 45° chamfer on the back edges on the box tops and bottoms to clear for the hinges.

## Make the Ends

Resaw a bit of cherry to make the ends. It is far safer to resaw a length of 15" or 16" using the table saw so the piece can be grabbed safely from the other side of the blade. Cut the ends for these boxes on the band saw, and plane them to ⁵⁄₁₆" thick.

## Glue the Ends in Place

Lightly sand the inside edges before gluing on the ends. Spread glue on the ends of the bottom pieces and then clamp the end pieces in place with a bar clamp, using clamping blocks to avoid marring the wood.

## Trim the Lid to Fit

After the glue has dried, trim the lid a very slight amount shorter – a hair from each end – to give side clearance for opening the box.

## Insert the Hinges

Insert the hinges with just a bit of glue in the holes, and then sand the top, sides and ends flush on the 6" x 48" belt sander. Start with a coarse grit to bring the surfaces even, moving to a finer grit before sanding the inlay flush with the lid. Before orbital sanding, use the chamfering bit in the router table to lightly chamfer the ends of the boxes, sand with the inverted orbital sander, and finish with three coats of Danish oil.

# ZERO-CLEARANCE INSERT

The zero-clearance insert for the table saw is an essential item for ripping thin stock to make inlay. I had been using one for about 20 years, without knowing what to call it, when I saw a magazine article mentioning it. The purpose of the zero-clearance insert is to give better support to thin stock that might slip down into a standard insert, creating a dangerous situation for the woodworker. It also helps prevent tear-out on the underside of the board. You will find, in operating a table saw, that the mass of the workpiece is inversely related to smoothness of the cutting operation. When you cut a piece of wood thinner and thinner through a number of ripping operations, the piece will begin to chatter and feel less certain to the operator. It is when the workpiece reaches the thinner stages, and the stock is least well supported by the saw table that the zero-clearance insert becomes most necessary. I make my zero-clearance inserts of maple. I usually make several blanks at a time because these are disposable items.

I plane maple stock down to the thickness of the recessed area of the table saw top, and then clamp a guide template on it and rout it with a template-following router bit. With the insert blank in place, I turn the saw on and gradually raise the blade as it cuts through the insert. A good safety measure is to cover a portion of the insert, with the fence of the saw table clamped in place on the side of the insert, just away from where the blade will raise through. This will enable you to give your full attention to the matter of slowly raising the blade.

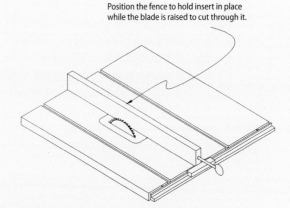

Position the fence to hold insert in place while the blade is raised to cut through it.

# CHAPTER FOUR

# TRIANGLE BOX

This is a very simple box that is artistic and easy to make. It is made of black walnut and inlaid with spalted maple, or it could be inlaid attractively with the triangle pattern from the koa box (chapter two). As it is difficult to glue end grain without mechanical fasteners – dovetails, splines, finger joints, screws or nails – the triangle box is made with the grain running vertically, giving good opportunity for successful gluing without making the project very complicated.

## MATERIALS LIST

| Plywood or particle board | | ¼" (for making a jig) |
|---|---|---|
| Baltic birch plywood | | ⅛" (for the bottom) |
| Walnut | | ¾" x 3¼" x 13" |
| Spalted maple for inlay | | |
| Bottom | 1 pc. | ⅛" x 2⁹⁄₁₅" (each side) |
| Spalted inlay | 2 pcs. | 1½" x 6¼" (size to fit) |
| Sides | 2 pcs. | 3¼" x 3" x 6" |
| Top | 1 pc. | ⅞" x 3³⁄₁₆" (each side) |

## TOOLS LIST

| |
|---|
| Band saw |
| Jointer |
| Router table |
| Planer |
| Table saw |
| 1" straight-cut bit |
| ¹⁄₁₆"-radius roundover bit |
| chamfering bit |

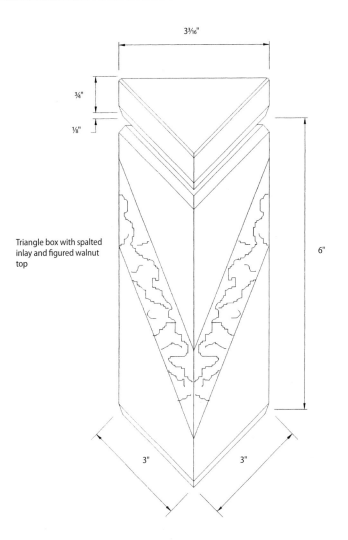

Triangle box with spalted inlay and figured walnut top

# MAKING THE TRIANGLE BOX

## Prepare the Stock
Start by resawing 4/4 walnut stock right down the middle on the band saw, and then plane the material to about ¼" thick. Joint one edge of the stock on the jointer before ripping it to the desired width on the table saw. Next cut three equal lengths of stock.

## Make the Angled Inlay Guide
Make a guide for routing the angled channel for the diagonal inlay to fit. Take a piece of ¼" plywood scrap, and laying the piece of wood that you intend to inlay on top of it at the angle you want, trace around the wood with a pencil. Then use the band saw to cut the shape out of the scrap wood, so that the scrap wood becomes a guide for carrying the workpiece along the router table fence to rout the inlay channel.

## Cut the Inlay Channel
After completing the guide piece, set up the router so that the height of the 1" straight-cut bit is just a bit

**1**

Make an angled inlay guide by taking a piece of ¼" plywood scrap, and laying the piece of wood that you plan to inlay on top of it at the angle intended. Trace around the wood with a pencil. Cut away the waste with the band saw.

2

The scrap wood becomes a guide for carrying the workpiece along the fence to rout the channel for the inlay. Rout one side with the guide piece face down; turn the guide piece over to rout the other piece.

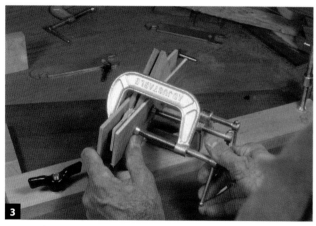

3

Because the two sides mirror each other, glue them up at the same time, clamping them together with blocking between.

lower than the thickness of the inlay. Adjust the fence to position the cutter so that it will cut the channel in the workpiece, using the guide piece you've made. Rout the first piece with the guide piece moving along the fence and the workpiece held firmly by hand pressure on the guide. To reverse the pattern for the adjoining workpiece, turn the guide end over end and rout the second piece. The two front pieces of the box will be mirror images of each other. If you want to widen the channel to accommodate wider inlay, move the fence away from the cutter and perform the two operations again.

## Install the Inlay

Next, size the inlay pieces to fit (as described in making the simple inlay box in chapter one). Cut the angled pieces oversized in length using the miter guide on the table saw. Select the pattern carefully so that the two angled sides appear related in color and pattern, and then glue the pieces in place. Put a thin strip of wood between the two sides and backing pieces to prevent marring from the C-clamps, making a sandwich with the inlay pieces and backing in the middle.

## MAKING THE ANGLED SIDES

### Trim the Inlay

After the glue holding the inlay in place has dried, trim the spalted wood even with the walnut using a flush-laminate trimming bit in the router. Place the inlaid parts facedown on the router table and use the guide beating on the bit to follow the walnut, leaving the spalted wood flush with the walnut edge.

### Cut the Angled Sides

To cut the pieces so that their angles intersect requires a simple jig, because table saws do not tilt to cut a 30° angle with the workpiece flat on the table. I made a jig that follows the miter slot in the table saw to hold the workpiece vertical as it slides through the saw. Set the angle of the saw at 60°, and clamp the workpiece in place on the jig so that one edge is flush with the surface of the table saw. Cut one edge and then the other of the three pieces that form the sides of the box. Of course, it is a good idea to cut test pieces to check the exact intersection of the angles rather than ruin nicely inlaid parts.

### Cut the Groove for the Bottom

After the angles have been cut, set up the crosscut table on the table saw, adjust the blade height to only about ⅛", and set a stop-block to position a ⅛" dado cut, which will hold the bottom panel. Make this cut about ¼" from the bottom edges of the parts.

### Make the Bottom

For the bottom use ⅛" Baltic birch plywood, and cut it to shape on the band saw. Cut it deliberately under-sized to allow for the contraction of the box body during the dry seasons. Measure the length of the dado cut across the side parts to determine the dimensions of the bottom, with each side of the triangle being a bit less than the length of the dado cut.

## ASSEMBLING THE BOX

### Round the Edges
Use a ¹⁄₁₆" roundover bit in the router to put a smooth edge on the inside edges of the body of the box; lightly hand sand these edges with #240-grit sandpaper.

### Apply Glue and Assemble
Spread glue on each edge, position the bottom in place and hold the three pieces together. Use rubber bands as clamps to apply pressure to the joints, and leave them in place as the glue dries.

## MAKING THE TOP

### Transfer the Angle to the Top
Make the top out of crotch-figured black walnut. Cut and plane a piece to about ⅞" thick. Use a sliding T-bevel to transfer the 60° angle from the assembled box to the wood for the top (marking the size just a bit larger than the size of the box), and then cut out the top.

### Cut the Lip for the Lid
After the top is cut to shape, sand away the saw marks using the belt sander. Set up the router table with the straight-cut bit to cut the lip where the lift-off lid fits into the box body.

## SANDING & FINISHING
Sand the outside surfaces of the box on the belt sander, bringing the inlay flush with the walnut sides and moving from #100-grit to #150-grit. Rout the bottom edge, the top edge and the lid with a 45° chamfering bit on the router. Orbital sand through #180-, #240- and #320-grits. Hand sand the corners of the box to take off the sharp feel. Finish with three coats of Danish oil.

**4**

The flush-trim router bit makes quick work of trimming the inlay.

**5**

This jig enables you to cut the sides at 30°. This is not possible using the settings on your table saw.

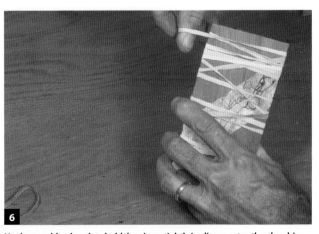

**6**

Use large rubber bands to hold the pieces tightly in alignment as the glue dries.

# CHAPTER FIVE

# BRACELET BOX WITH SPALTED MAPLE INLAY

This bracelet box derived from the simple inlaid box (chapter one), was the presentation box for a Christmas present for my wife, Jean, in 1995. The gift, a beaded bracelet with warm earth-toned glass beads and a clasp of natural amber, was made by a friend of mine, Eleanor Lux. I decided that the best way to wrap it would be in a walnut box, so I designed this quick presentation box. Jean likes it as much as her beautiful bracelet. You can modify its appearance through the use of any of the inlay techniques shown in this book. You can easily modify its size to fit the presentation needs of a particular piece of jewelry.

## MATERIALS LIST

**Walnut**

| Top and bottom | 2 pcs. | ¾" x 1¾" x 8½" |
|---|---|---|
| Ends | 2 pcs. | 5/16" x 1¼" x 1⅞" |

**Spalted maple**

| Inlay | 1 pc. | 3/32" x 1⅜" x 9" |
|---|---|---|

## TOOLS LIST

| Stationary belt sander |
|---|
| Standard ⅛"-kerf finish-cut blade |
| Thin-kerf finish-cut blade |
| Router table with ¾" or 1" straight-cut bit |
| 45° chamfering bit |
| C-clamps and one bar clamp |
| Table saw |

# MAKING THE BOX

## Cut the Inlay

Cut the inlay from a block of spalted maple using a thin-kerf 50-tooth blade, which gives a very smooth cut. To avoid chattering of the thin stock, use a zero-clearance insert in the opening of the table saw. This securely supports the inlay strips as they are cut. Never cut short pieces of spalted material in this manner, as short pieces are much more dangerous to handle. It is safer to cut them on the band saw and sand the surface that's to be glued.

## Make the Top

To make the lift-off lid, cut a piece of walnut the same width as the base, using a pivoting jig mounted to the band saw to cut a smooth curve. The base of the jig is clamped to the table of the band saw, while the upper part pivots on a 23" radius. After sawing the lid to shape, sand it on the 6" x 48" belt sander. At this point in sanding, you are not aiming for a perfect finish, but rather for a smooth contour for inlaying. The coarse sanding marks will actually be helpful later on in making sure that you do not sand through the inlay.

## Make the Base

Make this box in much the same way as the simple inlaid box (chapter one). Define the interior space with a series of saw-kerfs about 9/16" deep, slightly wider than the bracelet.

1

The thin-kerf blade gives a smooth surface for gluing, with very little waste.

2

Use a jig made for the band saw to cut the top to its curved shape. This jig is clamped to the band saw table and pivots on a wide radius, giving a smooth curve for bending the inlay.

Finish shaping the top on the belt sander by rocking the workpiece and checking frequently to make sure you are sanding evenly. The band saw marks help to gauge your progress.

Use either a dado blade or a series of ⅛" saw cuts to cut away the inside of the box, and then widen the opening by making a 15° cut on each side.

With the saw still at a 15° angle, lower the blade and adjust the fence to cut the top to fit the opening in the base.

With the lid turned on edge and the saw returned to 90°, cut away the remaining edge so the lid fits into the base.

Then make angled cuts at about 15° off perpendicular to widen the opening so that the bracelet does not appear to be in a deep hole, allowing more light to illuminate the beads.

## Fit the Lid

With the blade still set at the 15° angle, but lowered to a height of ⅛", reset the fence to cut the edges of the top to fit exactly into the opening in the base. With the table saw returned to 90°, and the lid on edge against the fence, cut away the remaining edge.

## INLAYING THE CURVED TOP

### Cut the Channel in the Top

Cutting the channel is done much the same way as inlaying a flat surface on the router, but cut it thinner in order for it to bend more easily to the radius of the top. Raise the cutter almost to the thickness of the inlay you plan to use, and then clamp two pieces of thin wood both before and after the cutter. These form a cradle to control the rocking movement of the top as the inlay channel is cut.

### Size the Inlay

When the channel is cut, size the inlay piece in the same manner as for the simple inlaid box in chapter one.

### Install the Inlay

Gluing the inlay piece in place requires a special clamping arrangement. Take the piece of wood that was left over when the top was sawn and cut it on the table saw to about ⅛" narrower than the finished piece of inlay. Use this piece and a backing piece of ⅛"-thick plywood to provide a flat place for the C-clamps to grip and to evenly distribute clamping pressure. Use a piece of scrap wood on the opposite side to prevent the C-clamps from marring the wood. This arrangement, using three or four C-clamps per box top, will provide plenty of clamping pressure.

## FINAL ASSEMBLY

### Sand the Top

With a sheet of fine sandpaper and working on a very flat surface (the top of the table saw or a smooth workbench), sand the top surfaces of the box body. Then sand the sharp edges, both inside the box and on the outside where they will intersect the lid, slightly round. To match the edge of the box body, lightly sand the edges of the lid with a fine-grit sandpaper to match the sanded edge on the box bottom.

### Glue Up the Parts

Using a technique similar to the one used to assemble the simple inlaid box in chapter one, spread glue on the ends of the shaped box body and clamp the end pieces in place with a bar clamp while the glue sets. Unlike the simple inlaid box, the ends of this box are cut tall

**7** Here's the fit you are looking for.

**8** Clamp thin stock on the router table to help cradle the lid as you rout the channel for the inlay. Notice the thin piece of wood behind my hand forming the front half of the cradle.

**9** After making one edge true on the jointer, pass the strip between the cutter and fence on the router table to size it to fit in the lid. The safety blocking that would normally cover the bit has been removed to show the process.

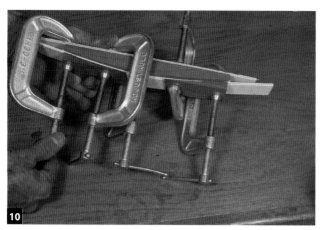

**10**

Use the cutoffs from shaping the lid along with a strip of Baltic birch to obtain even clamping pressure.

**11**

After gluing end pieces on the base, hold the top and bottom together for sanding on the belt sander, using the coarse sanding marks left in forming the box shape as a guide to ensure that you are sanding evenly – but not through – the inlay. When the coarse sanding marks are gone, you have sanded enough.

enough to cover the end grain of the lid and give it a resting place when the box is closed.

## Trim the Top

Cut the box lid about 1/64" shorter than the inside length of the box. To avoid overcutting and making the lid too loose, clamp a stop-block on the cutoff box, cut the box lid to length and check the fit, bumping it over very slightly away from the stop-block if it needs to be shorter. The stop-block provides a secure frame of reference to keep from cutting away too much.

## Final Sanding

When the box top is fitted to the box bottom, hold the pieces together and sand them as a unit on the 6" x 48" belt sander. This quickly shapes the ends to conform to the lid. Because the inlay is thinner than usual, you have to be careful not to sand through: Use the coarse sanding markings to ensure that the inlay is not becoming too thin. When the coarse sanding marks are gone, you have sanded enough.

## Rout the Edges

Use a 45° chamfering bit in the router to add interest to the edges, routing all edges except the top edge of the ends.

## Finishing

Finish the box by rubbing with three coats of Danish oil.

# CHAPTER SIX

# WALNUT BOX WITH SPALTED MAPLE INLAY

This box is one of my current production pieces; I do these in a variety of sizes for sale through galleries nationwide. It is my basic box, which has evolved over a number of years from the simple inlaid box in chapter one. It has a sloping lid – which adds interest to the design, but also serves the very practical purpose of saving wood while allowing appropriate thickness at the rear of the box for the use of miniature barrel hinges. The spalted maple inlay comes from wood that friends have given me, I have milled myself with a chain saw or a friend milled with a portable sawmill, and that's been dried in another friend's greenhouse. In a way, my use of spalted woods is a community effort. Over the years, I've had wood delivered to me by a friend on the parks commission, and the mayor has called to offer me wood from trees fallen along the city streets. Once when a spalted maple had fallen on power lines in front of a home here in Eureka Springs, I was away at a show and friends arranged for a front end loader to lift it and a truck to haul it to my home. It seems sometimes that the wood gathers faster than I can use it, especially when it is cut in ⅛"-thick strips for inlay. My use of spalted woods is an important part of my work: I enjoy revealing this hidden beauty of our forests. I usually mill it about 2½" thick. This is a reasonable thickness for me to cut on the table saw without too much strain, and it allows some flexibility for use beyond making boxes; for instance, resawing it into panels for small cabinets, drawer facings on chests and other uses. I dry the wood for about a year in the warm and dry conditions of an abandoned, plantless greenhouse before using it. This box is made with mortise-and-tenon joints and a floating panel bottom. It is made to last through many years of seasonal changes in humidity.

## MATERIALS LIST

| Black walnut | | 1" x 3" x 20" |
|---|---|---|
| Spalted maple for inlay | | |
| Miniature barrel hinges | 4 pcs. | |
| Fronts and backs | 4 pcs. | 1⁵⁄₁₆" x 3⁷⁄₈" |
| Ends | 4 pcs. | 2⁹⁄₁₆" x 2⅛" |
| Bottoms | 2 pcs. | 2¹⁄₁₆" x 3¹⁹⁄₃₂" |

## TOOLS LIST

Band saw

Planer

Router table

1" and ⅛" straight-cut router bits

⅛" and ¹⁄₁₆" roundover bits

6"X 48" belt sander

Drill press with 5mm brad-point bit

Jointer

Table saw

Orbital sander

## MAKING THE BOX

### Prepare the Materials

Cut a 4½" piece off the end of the 20" piece of walnut; this piece will be resawn later into the lids for two boxes. Resaw the 20" piece of walnut on the band saw, using a fence set so that the blade cuts right down the middle. This gives you pieces thick enough to be planed to ⁵⁄₁₆" thick. From this stock, cut fronts, backs, ends and bottoms with the dimensions shown in the materials list.

### Mortise the End Pieces

Your next step is to mortise the ends for the front, back and bottom to fit. Do this with a ⅛" router bit mounted in the router table. Adjust the bit to cut to a depth of just more than ⅛", and check your test piece with a dial caliper. (I prefer that the depth be just barely over ⁸⁄₆₄" to accommodate any variances and allow a space for excess

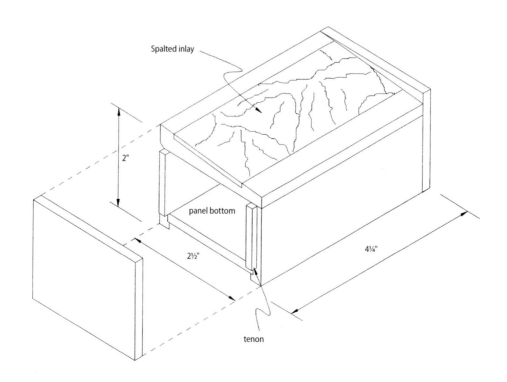

Spalted inlay

2"

panel bottom

2½"

4¼"

tenon

When resawing on the band saw, watch to ensure your blade is tracking well so you end up with two pieces of equal thickness.

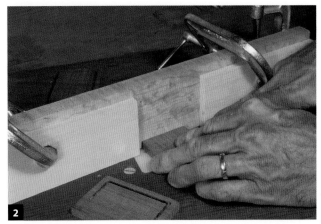

Stop-blocks on the fence ensure the mortises will be the correct length.

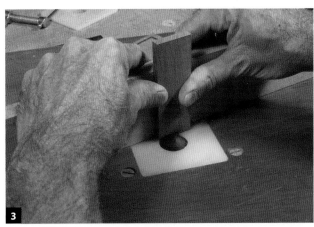

Cut the tenons using the router table with fence and a 1" straight-cut router bit. The bit I use has a slight twist in the cutting edges, which gives it a very clean and smooth cut. Here, the safety blocking has been removed to show the operation.

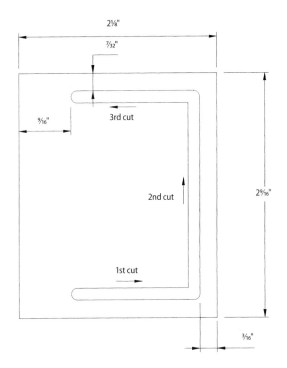

2⅛"

7/32"

9/16"

3rd cut

2nd cut

2 9/16"

1st cut

3/16"

glue when the box is assembled.) Set the fence on the router table so that the outside edge of the cutter is ¹¹/₃₂". When the ⁵/₁₆" sides are in place, this allows ¹/₃₂" to sand level with the sides. Check this measurement with the dial caliper as well, using a test piece. Use stop-blocks clamped to the fence to control the length of the mortises. Set up for a test piece, and when you have set up for the right travel of the workpiece to rout the first mortise, cut the mortises in all the ends, positioning each piece between the stops. Press the workpiece down onto the cutter, moving the piece right to left and then left to right to clear the mortise of sawdust. Finally lift it off the cutter. Leaving the fence in position, adjust the stop-blocks

A good friction fit tells you your tenon is the right size.

Use the table saw and a blade with a ⅛" kerf to cut the dados ⅛" x ⅛" where the bottom panels fit the front and back pieces.

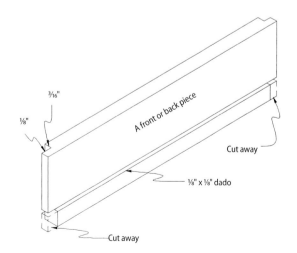

3/16"

⅛"

A front or back piece

Cut away

⅛" x ⅛" dado

Cut away

Using the cutoff box, cut away the nubs on the ends of the front and back pieces.

on the fence to rout the second mortise on all the ends. Then set up and rout the last mortise on all the ends. You will note that this sequence involves making only one plunge cut on the router table on each end piece, with the subsequent cut starting where the last cut ended.

## Cut the Tenons

Cutting the mortises first allows you to check the tenons and adjust them for the best possible fit. To cut the tenons, use the router table with fence and a 1" straight-cut router bit. The bit I use has a slight twist in the cutting edges, which gives it a very clean and smooth cut. Set the height of the cutter from the table at exactly ⅛". Then adjust the fence so that the distance from the inside edge of the cutter and the fence is ⅛". After these adjustments are made, clamp safety blocks onto the router table to prevent your fingers from having any access to the operating cutter. Cut a test piece standing up along the fence, and move it carefully from right to left. Checking the resulting tenon with the dial caliper tells you whether to raise or lower the cutter by slight increments to obtain tenons exactly ⅛" long. Check the fit of the tenon in the mortise, and move the fence in or out as necessary to obtain a good fit. For a good fit, I look for a tenon that will slip into the mortise without difficulty, but if I hold the mortised end upside down, is tight enough that there is enough friction that the tenoned piece does not fall out

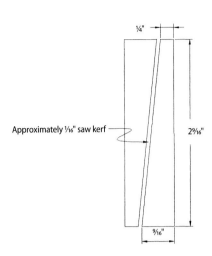

1/4"

Approximately 1/16" saw kerf

2 9/16"

9/16"

without shaking it. When you are satisfied with the tenon cut on the test piece, cut tenons on each end of the front and back pieces.

## Cut the Dados for the Bottom Panels

Set up the table saw with a 1/8"-kerf blade to cut the dados where the bottom panels fit the front and back pieces. Set the blade height so that the center of the cut is 1/8" deep and the fence is 1" from the blade. This will give the finished box 1" of interior height.

## Trim the Tenons

After cutting the dados, trim off the little nubs left between the dado and bottom edges. To do this, use the cutoff box on the table saw, with the blade raised just enough to cut the nubs off each end and with the stop-block adjusted so that the cut is flush with the surface left in tenoning.

## Make the Bottom Panels

Use the same router-table setup and settings as used for the tenons to cut the rabbeted edge on the bottom panels where they fit into the end pieces. In order to get a good fit where the panels fit into the dados on the fronts and backs, you usually will have to adjust the fence in or out. Notice that in cutting the ends of the panels and the tenons on the fronts and backs, the router setup calls for climb-feeding the stock into the cutter. This involves feeding the wood into the bit in the same direction the bit is turning. This gives a very clean cut when remov-

**7**

Use the router table and a 1" straight-cut router bit to cut the channel for the spalted inlay. Use the piece of inlay to help set up the height of cut, leaving the bit cutting less than the full thickness of the inlay.

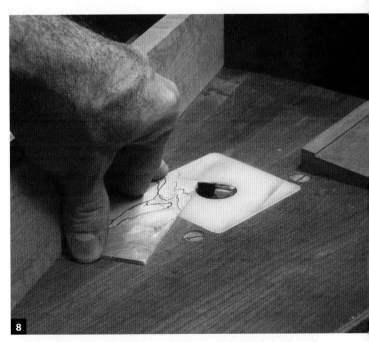

**8**

After cutting the channel to the planned width, size the inlay to fit the channel, raising the bit higher than the thickness of the inlay and adjusting the fence so that the opening equals the width of the channel in the lid. Use safety blocking for this operation.

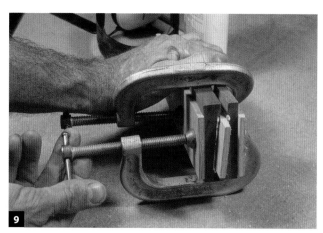

Glue two boxes at once to make clamping easier. Use a spacer between the boxes to keep the lids from gluing to each other and to distribute pressure evenly on the inlay. Additional blocking protects the undersides of the lids from the clamps.

Set up stop-blocks on the drill press for controlling the positions of the holes.

The position of the stop-blocks must be changed for the lids, moving the blocks in ⅛" on each side, because the lids are cut shorter than the tenoned fronts and backs.

ing end grain. A conventional feed, against the rotation of the bit, can cause unwanted tear-out. This operation requires a very firm hold on the workpiece. Safety blocking must be securely in place to prevent fingers from being pulled into the cutter. If you have not tried a cut like this before, practice with scraps until you feel comfortable with it. The danger is greatly increased when cutting very hard woods, like the tight grain that forms around knots. Climb-feeding is more likely to grab the wood and pull it into the cutter when cutting the rabbets on the sides of the panels, since the long grain does not shear away as easily as the end grain. This operation requires a very firm hand and very close attention. Never do this without safety blocking. Blocking will help prevent fingers from coming in contact with the router bit.

## Make the Lids

Plane the material for the tops to ⅞", joint it and rip it to just more than 2⁹⁄₁₆" wide, and then joint the ripsawn edge smooth. This gives you enough good stock to band saw the piece into two tops. Rather than set the saw to a particular angle, mark the angle on the end of the workpiece with a line measured as in the drawing below. Then adjust the band saw table to the angle marked on the end of the workpiece. Test that the angle and the fence are set just right by cutting slightly into one end and then turning the piece over to see that the band saw blade slips perfectly into the cut. Then cut the piece into material for two box tops.

## Inlaying the Top

Select the inlay for the tops of the boxes and cut it to just more than the length of the lid. Then rout a channel in the tops, following the sequence described for making the simple inlaid box (chapter one). In the finished box, the spalted inlay will be surrounded equally on all sides by a walnut frame. For the 2½" top, with the frame to the right and left being formed by the end pieces (which are ⁵⁄₁₆" thick), the channel inlay will be routed to a width of 1⅞". Start by setting the height of the router bit to nearly the thickness of the inlay above the table, and set the fence so that the 1" straight-cut bit will cut a channel right down the middle of the top. Cut the channel on the band-sawn face. In successive cuts, widen the channel equally by moving the fence further away from the cutter and turning the workpiece end over end. When the cut nears the right width for the inlay piece make a final thin cut with the workpiece fed into the router in the opposite direction and the fence opening narrowed. This cut will ensure that the channel is uniform throughout its length, because both sides of the channel will be indexed from the same side.

## Install the Inlay

When the channel is finished, trim the inlay strip to fit using the router table and the techniques described for making the simple inlaid box (chapter one). Then glue the strips in place. Because the tops are cut at an angle, arrange them face to face, the way they were cut apart at the band saw, with a piece of scrap plywood between them and on the outside to obtain even pressure from the clamps and to prevent the clamps from marring what will be the inside of the lids.

## Fit the Lids

After the tops have been clamped long enough for the glue to set, put one of the boxes together without glue and trim the tops to the length of the inside space between the ends. I like the lids to be about 1/64" shorter than the opening. At this level of tolerance, I can just barely feel movement when I move the lid side to side in the assembled box. Use the cutoff box to accurately make this trim cut.

## Fit the Hinges

Drill the holes for the press-in-place barrel hinges with a 5mm brad-point drill bit in the drill press. Because the backs and lids are different heights and lengths, you have to change the depth of the drilling and the position of the stop-blocks to drill these parts. The setting of the fence remains constant. After drilling the holes, chamfer the back edges of the back and lid to clear for the operation of the lid.

Whenever I set up to use any new type of hardware, I play with it a bit to find out what its needs are and how to design and cut for its use. It can be very helpful to do a sample setup with the hinges and sample wooden parts.

## Sand the Inside Surfaces

Before final assembly, sand the inside surfaces and ends of the tops. It is easier to do this now than to wait until the box is assembled. Also, rout the outside top edge of the front pieces with a 1/16" roundover bit. This creates an obvious place for fingertips to open the finished box.

**12**
Be careful to use just enough glue to do the job without excess squeeze out.

**13**
Put just a drop of woodworker's glue into each of the hinge holes, slip the hinges into the holes on the lids, pushing them partially in place, align the lid with the base of the box and squeeze it into position. This is a good time to test the opening and closing of the lid, as this will let you know if the box is assembled square.

**14**
Set the band saw table at the same angle used to cut the lids, and cut the ends to match the shape of the top.

**15**

Use a ¹⁄₁₆" roundover bit to rout the front edge of the lid after sanding it on the belt sander.

## FINAL ASSEMBLY

Use a small squeeze bottle to apply glue to the insides of the mortises and the end pieces, then slip the fronts, backs and bottom panels in place. If you have obtained a good fit in cutting the tenons, the boxes will go together easily and not need clamping. If the fit is just a little bit loose, rubber bands or tape will do the trick. Before the glue has set, it is good to check the bottom panels to ensure that the spacing is uniform and to make necessary corrections. This is also the time to press the hinges in place and to attach the lids. Slip the hinges into the holes on the lids with just a drop of woodworker's glue. Then push them partially in place, line them up with the holes on the back sides of the boxes and press them firmly into place until the hinges have seated. Installing the lids now allows you to make sure, while you still have time to adjust the fit, the boxes are square in relation to the lids and that they open and close smoothly. If the lid rubs when opening and closing the box, squeeze it corner to corner just a bit to square the box to the lid.

### Trim the Ends

After the glue has dried, trim the excess wood from the ends. Use the band saw, with the table tilted so that the blade travels parallel to the face of the box and the fence to allow the completed box to pass between the fence and blade with just a small cleanup allowance.

### Sanding

Sand the box on the 6" x 48" belt sander, starting with #80-grit to sand the inlay, ends and top flush. Use the band saw markings and their gradual disappearance as your guide to even sanding; this way, you avoid sanding through the layer of inlay. Then change the belt to #100- or #120-grit and sand all surfaces of the box smooth. Finish the belt sanding with #150-grit.

### Rout the Box Edges

Before the final sanding, use the router with the ¹⁄₁₆" roundover bit installed to round the front inside edge of the lid to match the contour of the front piece. Then mount a ¹⁄₈" roundover bit and rout all the edges of the box except the top front edge of the lid.

### Final Finish

Orbital sand all sides of the boxes with a progression of grits from #180 to #240 and #320. With each sanding, gently round the front edge, sanding the corners as well as the flat surfaces. Use a holder clamped to the workbench to avoid the fatigue of using a large orbital sander. Finish the box with three coats of Danish oil.

# ROUTER TABLE SAFETY

One of the things that make the router a relatively safe tool is that generally, while it's in use, both hands are placed firmly on its handles. When using a router inverted in a router table, it becomes infinitely more dangerous unless special care is taken in setting up guards to keep the fingers out of the way of the moving router bit. Because I use the router for so many diverse operations, it is not practical to have a safety guard that is useful in all the various setups. I have found it fast and convenient to make safety blocking from various pieces of scrap wood clamped in place on the surface of the router table.

The router table becomes even more dangerous when using a technique called climb-feeding, which means that the router is turning in a direction that self-feeds – like a radial arm saw – pulling the wood into the cut. This technique can give a smoother cut with less likelihood of tear-out, but at greater risk to you, because the router bit can grab the wood and pull it (and your fingers) into the cut. The danger of climb-feeding is reduced when cutting end grain and soft woods and is proportionate to the size of the cut. The danger increases with a dull router bit cutting along the grain, or on particularly hard pieces of wood, like figured walnut. It is extremely important in all cases to use safety blocking to prevent serious injury when making a climb-feed cut.

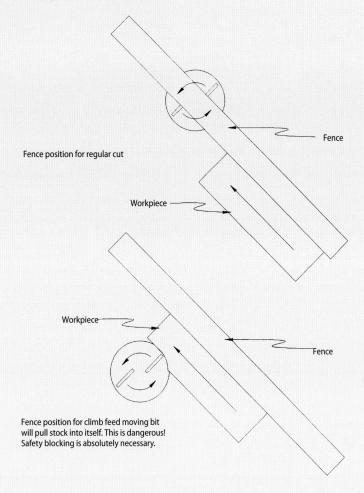

Fence position for regular cut

Fence

Workpiece

Workpiece

Fence

Fence position for climb feed moving bit will pull stock into itself. This is dangerous! Safety blocking is absolutely necessary.

# CHAPTER SEVEN

# CHECKERBOARD INLAY BOX

This box is made of curly sugar maple with inlay of walnut and fiddleback soft maple. It is a good size to use as a place to gather all the stuff that collects in your pockets during the day: pens, pencils, pocket knives, keys and so on. Its angled ends and sides and the checkerboard inlay give it a very contemporary look. Its mortise-and-tenon craftsmanship will allow it to last through many years of use. The angled resawing technique uses materials efficiently.

## MATERIALS LIST

| 5/4 curly sugar maple | | 3" x 16" |
|---|---|---|
| Brass pins | 2 pcs. | 3/16" (cut from brass welding rod) |
| Ends | 2 pcs. | 3⅝" x 3" |
| Sides | 2 pcs. | 1¾" x 6⅜" |
| Bottom | 1 pc. | ⅛" x 2¼" x 6⅜" (birch plywood) |
| Top | 1 pc. | ½" x 2⅝" x 6" (before final trimming) |

## TOOLS LIST

| |
|---|
| Band saw |
| Table saw |
| Jointer |
| Planer |
| Router table |
| Orbital sander |
| ⅛" roundover bit |
| ⅛" and ¾" or 1" straight-cut bit |
| Stationary belt sander |
| 45° chamfering bit |
| Tapered sanding disc |

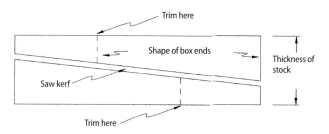

Slide cut outs of these shapes to determine the width of stock needed to cut ends from given thickness of material.

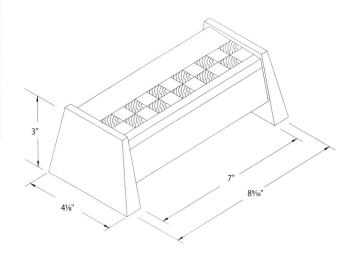

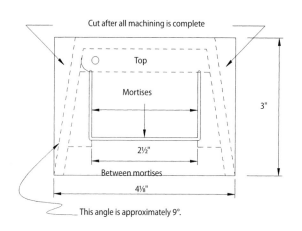

# MAKING THE BOX

## Resaw the Stock

While the outside of this box consists of angled planes, the inside shape is rectangular, with 90° sides. To make this box, resaw wood on the band saw for the sides and ends at a 9° or 10° angle. The exact degree of the angle is not critical to the success of this project. Mark the shape of the box end on the end of the board, tilt the band saw table to align with that mark, cut into the end of the stock and turn it over to see that the saw is cutting into the exact center. If not, adjust the fence in or out as necessary. If 5/4 stock is not available, plan your cutting so that parts overlap (keeping waste to a minimum). This requires wider stock to form the parts, but is still thrifty when using fine woods. To figure the size of stock needed, sketch the shape of the resawn, finished-size stock. Cut out two pieces of paper in that shape and slide them in relation to each other until they fit within the thickness of the stock (allowing 3/16" between them for the

A run through your disc sander will cut down on sanding time later.

Using a square and a sliding T-bevel, mark the mortises and the cut lines on a sample end piece, and rout the mortises in the same way end pieces are formed for the walnut box with spalted maple inlays in chapter six.

After routing the mortises, cut the end pieces to shape using the cutoff table on the table saw with a guide strip tacked in place. The sliding T-bevel is very useful for setting up the desired angle.

band saw kerf and cleanup allowance). Use the same angle to resaw the stock for the fronts and backs of the box, but you can use narrower stock to come out with the right width for these parts.

## Sand the Resawn Pieces

After the stock is resawn, run it through a tapered disc sander on the table saw to cut down on your sanding time later and to remove the band saw marks.

## Lay Out the Mortises on the End Pieces

The ends are not cut to final shape until they have been machined to fit the other parts. Cut them to length, as shown on page 47, and then lay out the exact positions of the mortises for the front, back and bottom pieces with a sliding T-bevel, a pencil and a square. The angled lines shown are transferred from the shape of the angled stock, using the sliding T-bevel.

## Cut the Mortises

To form the mortises in this box, use the same procedure described for mortising the ends of the walnut box with spalted maple inlay in the previous chapter, with the following differences. Set the height of the $\frac{1}{8}$"cutter at $\frac{3}{16}$" above the router table. Check with a dial caliper when making a test mortise. I am satisfied with the depth when it is just more than $\frac{12}{64}$". Set the fence so that the position of the mortise will allow for waste to be trimmed from the end pieces after assembly.

Rout the mortises for the front and back pieces first. These require the same fence setting, but different settings for the stop-blocks. Then adjust the fence to cut the mortise for the bottom panel to fit, cutting between the mortises you have already cut for the front and back.

## Cut the Tenons for the Front and Back Pieces

Cut the tenons for the front and back pieces to fit the end mortises exactly as you did for the walnut box with spalted inlay (chapter six), except that the tenon is cut to the exact length of $\frac{3}{16}$". Check the length of the tenon with the dial indicator. I am satisfied when it reads exactly $\frac{12}{64}$". Take special care cutting the tenons, due to the added thickness and shape of the front and back pieces, and fix safety blocks on the router table to keep your fingers clear of the cutter.

## Finish the Tenons

Cut the dados in the front and back pieces for the bottom panel to fit using the table saw with the blade height set to ⅛" and the distance of the blade from the fence at ⅛". Then cut the remaining nubs from the ends of the front and back pieces using the sliding cutoff table with a stop-block to guarantee the cut conforms to the routed cut forming the tenon.

## Make the Bottom

Cut the bottom from ⅛" Baltic birch plywood, checking the fit of the plywood in the mortises. If they are too tight, use the straight-cut bit in the router to size the stock to fit into the mortises in the end pieces while the router table is still set up from making the tenons. (Details of this procedure are described in chapter six.)

## Shape the Ends

After the machining operations on the ends are complete, set up the saw to trim the ends to final shape. I use a sliding cutoff table on the table saw, which unlike the normal cutoff table, does not have a fixed fence and allows simple cutting of complex shapes.

## Make the Channel for the Inlay

Rout the channel for the inlay to fit while the lid is still oversize in width and length, using the procedures described in chapter one. In this box, the inlay provides a point of reference that indicates where to open the box, so rout the channel on the side rather than centering it. A single narrow band placed in the center of the lid would lose its significance, and a wide band would hide too much of the curly pattern on the top.

## Dry-Assemble the Box and Trim the Top

After the inlay is complete and the clamps are removed, assemble the box without glue, measure the completed space between the ends and cut the top to fit the measured length. Check the fit: If it is tight, meaning that there is no side-to-side movement at all, then cut off just a tiny bit more on the table saw.

**4**

To determine the finished size of the top, assemble the box and mark the cut lines to trim the front and back edges at the angle that matches the front and back pieces, and then cut the lid to length to fit within the space allowed by the ends.

Using the cutoff box works very well for this. First, you know that the piece will come out square, and second, when using a stop-block, it is very easy to cut off just the right amount. Move the workpiece over until you see a very slight space, and then, holding the workpiece firmly in position, reclamp the stop-block against the workpiece.

# MAKING THE HINGES

## Bore Holes in the Top

This box uses a ³⁄₁₆" brass welding rod as hidden hinge pins. To form the hinges, drill ³⁄₁₆" holes in the ends of the lid. I use my old Shop Smith as a horizontal boring machine, using a ³⁄₁₆" drill and tilting the table parallel. To drill these holes with a conventional drill press, you could construct a jig to hold the stock on the table parallel to the bit, as shown in the drawing on page 50. Raise the table so that the drill will be centered in the workpiece. Set up a guide block to position the hole exactly where you want it, and use the fence to hold the workpiece in position. Drill a test piece, and check the location of the hole with the dial indicator. Drill to a depth of about ⅜", about ¹¹⁄₆₄" from the back edge and the inside surface of the top. Then set up the same arrangement to mill the other end of the top, once again testing the position of the hole with a test piece.

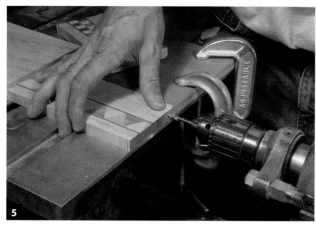

5

Use a horizontal borer for drilling the pin holes in the top. You can also use a jig on the drill press as shown in the drawing.

6

Drill holes for the hinge pins to fit into the ends with a ³⁄₁₆" brad-point bit. The opposite end, reversed and placed underneath, holds the workpiece square to the drill without changing the angle of the drill press table.

## Rout the Back Edge and Cut the Angles in the Lid

Rout the back edge of the lid with a ¼" roundover bit to give the lid clearance for opening. Then cut the lid to match the angles of the front and back pieces. Set up the saw, transferring the angle from the box front with the sliding T-bevel to set the angle of the saw blade. First trim the back edge to shape, taking care not to cut into the portion of the back edge shaped by the ¼" roundover, and then cut the front edge. An easy way to determine where to cut is to lay the lid in place on the dry-assembled box, use a straightedge to

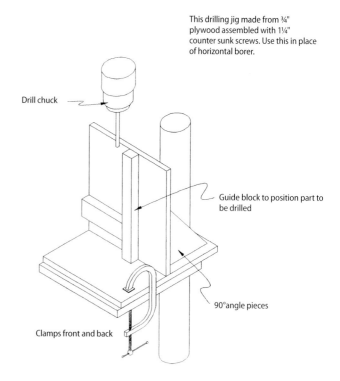

This drilling jig made from ¾" plywood assembled with 1¼" counter sunk screws. Use this in place of horizontal borer.

Drill chuck

Guide block to position part to be drilled

90°angle pieces

Clamps front and back

align the lid with the box back and then use a pencil to mark a cut line along the front edge of the lid.

## Drill Hinge-Pin Holes in the End Pieces

To drill the hinge-pin holes in the end pieces, first locate the positions for the holes while the box is dry-assembled. Use a steel rule laid against the angled back and mark the angle on the inside of the ends. Use this marking as a point from which to measure the location for the hinge-pin holes to be drilled, remembering to allow ¹⁄₃₂" clearance between the lid and box back for the lid to open. Use a matching piece with the same angle, reversed, to hold the end piece in proper relation to the drill.

## MAKING THE HINGE PINS

### Cut the Brass to Length

You can cut the brass hinge pins with a hacksaw, but because I usually cut the pins for several boxes at a time, I use an old carbide blade in the table saw and the sliding cutoff table. Set the stop-block a distance from the blade determined by adding the depth of the hinge hole in the end pieces and the depth of the holes drilled in the tops, less 1/64". Lower the blade so that it does not cut all the way through the rod, leaving just a little to break off by hand. This helps avoid having the piece break off while being cut and consequently be thrown by the saw. (I wear a face shield while cutting the pins just in case this should happen.)

## Clean Up the Pin Ends
After the pins are cut to length, sand the ends by rolling the pins against the stationary belt sander with your fingers. This step helps the box assembly go more smoothly.

## FINISHING TOUCHES

### Rout the Edges
Rout all edges with a 45° chamfering bit. Use the same setting to rout the ends and bottom edges of the front and back. Lower the bit to rout a smaller chamfer on the top edges of the front and back. Use a 1/8" roundover bit to rout the inside edges of the front and back.

### Sanding
Sand all the parts of this box prior to assembly, proceeding through the usual sequence of grits: #180, #240 and #320. Use an orbital sander inverted in a holder mounted on the workbench to make this job easier. The small chamfered edges are much easier to sand by hand with a sanding block: This will avoid unintended rounding of edges, keeping the lines of the box crisp and clean.

## FINAL ASSEMBLY

### Install the Hinge Pins in the Lid and Glue Up the Front and Back
After placing the hinge pins in the lid, apply glue with a squeeze bottle to the insides of the end mortises. Then put the front, back, bottom pieces and lid in place on one end. Using a piece of folded-over business card stock, shim the opposite end of the lid in position and place the other end piece in place. If your tenons are cut just right, the box will hold together without clamps.

After routing all the pieces and sanding each one to #320-grit, put glue in the mortises and assemble the box. Opening and closing the lid will indicate if the box is square and clearances are adequate.

### Check the Fit of the Lid
Check that the box is square by opening and closing the lid and observing its fit. If the lid rubs on one side, squeeze it from corner to corner, and check the lid operation again. If necessary, clamp the box together, using cushion blocks cut at the same angle as the sides and fronts to give even clamping pressure.

### Finish the Box
Finish the box in the usual manner with three coats of Danish oil.

# CHAPTER EIGHT

# SCULPTED PECAN BOX

This box, with its secret drawer, sculpted pecan lid and walnut pull, is very
similar in its construction techniques to the box in chapter seven: It is constructed with mortise-and-tenon joints. It differs in that the checkerboard inlaid
box is finish sanded prior to assembly, while this one is sanded after. The inspiration
for this box comes from the hills and valleys surrounding my home in the Ozark
Mountains. Our forest takes its shape from the underlying landscape, which is more
clearly revealed in early November when the leaves fall. The Ozark Mountains are
not mountains in the technical sense, like the Rockies or the Appalachians, but
have been formed through erosion by the movement of water on a huge plateau over
millions of years. I form the shape of the lid by "eroding" hollows from the central
plateau of the pecan lid with the belt sander. This very imprecise operation depends
on the skill and vision of the craftsperson.

## MATERIALS LIST

| 5/4 walnut | | 3" x 12" |
|---|---|---|
| Figured pecan | | ¾" x 3⅜" x 6" |
| Baltic birch | | ⅛" x 6¼" x 7" (for box and drawer bottoms) |
| Sugar maple | | A few sq. inches (for drawer sides) |
| Ends | 2 pcs. | 3" x 4" |
| Front and back | 2 pcs. | 2¼" x 6⅜" |
| Top | 1 pc. | ¾" x 3⅜" x 6" |
| Bottom | 1 pc. | ⅛" x 3" x 6⅜" |
| *Drawer* | | |
| Bottom | 1 pc. | ⅛" x 3⅛" 6³⁄₁₆" |
| Sides | 2 pcs. | ⁵⁄₁₆" x ½" x 5¹⁵⁄₁₆" |
| Back | 1 pc. | ⁵⁄₁₆" x ½" x 2¹¹⁄₁₆" |

## TOOLS LIST

| Table saw |
|---|
| Band saw |
| Router table |
| Drill press |
| Stationary belt sander |
| Orbital sander |

## MAKING THE BOX

I make this box with walnut ends and sides, and use pecan for the lid. This is an excellent use for figured wood or even disfigured wood that displays knots and other imperfections.

### Resaw the Walnut Stock

While the outside angles of the box are approximately 9°, the inside shape is rectangular with 90° sides. To make this box, resaw wood on the band saw at about a 9° angle for the sides and ends. Use the same techniques to shape the sides and ends of this box as used to make the checkerboard inlay box in chapter seven. All of the parts for this box can be resawn at the same time or, to save material, the front and back pieces can be cut from narrower stock. After the stock is resawn, use a sanding disc on the table saw to bring the resawn stock to its finished dimension.

### Rout the Mortises

To form the mortises in this box, use the same procedure described for mortising the ends of the walnut box with spalted maple inlay (chapter six), with the follow-

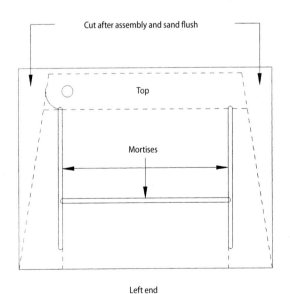

Left end

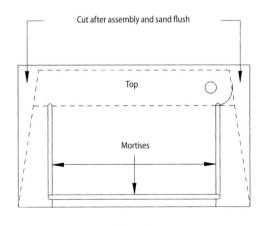

Right end

Use the cutoff box to trim the tenons on the front and back pieces. Note that these tenons are cut to allow for the hidden drawer.

Box front and backs

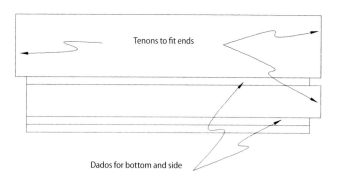
Tenons to fit ends

Dados for bottom and side

This shows the parts mortised, tenoned and nearly ready to assemble.

ing differences. Set the height of the ⅛" cutter at ³⁄₁₆" above the router table. When making a test mortise, check with a dial caliper; I am satisfied with the depth when it is just barely more than ¹²⁄₆₄". Set the fence so that the position of the mortise will allow for waste to be trimmed from the end pieces after assembly. Use the same fence setting to rout the mortises for both ends of the box, but change the positions of the stop-blocks for routing the opposite sides and opposite ends – a total of four separate setups. The left and right ends of this box are different: One end has a secret drawer and the other does not. Adjust the fence to cut the mortises for the bottom panel: A single setup will cut the mortises for both ends if indexed from the top edge.

## Cut the Tenons

Cutting the tenons for the front and back pieces to fit the end mortises is done exactly as for making the walnut box with spalted inlay, except that the tenon is cut to the exact length of ³⁄₁₆" to fit the mortise cut for it. Using a test piece, check the length of the tenon with the dial caliper, making sure it reads exactly ¹²⁄₆₄". As in making the checkerboard inlay box, take special care in cutting the tenons, due to the added thickness and shape of the front and back pieces, and fix safety blocks on the router table to keep your fingers clear of the cutter.

## Cut for the Drawer and Bottom to Fit

Use the table saw with a ⅛" blade raised to cut ⅛" deep to cut saw-kerfs for the bottom panel to fit. To cut for the secret drawer to fit, raise the blade to ³⁄₁₆" and change the position of the fence.

Next, trim away the nubs to allow the front and back pieces to fit the mortised ends. The drawing at the top of this page shows the cuts for the bottom and drawer guide, and where to trim the nubs.

## Make and Install the Hinges

Like the checkerboard inlay box, this box uses a ³⁄₁₆" brass welding rod for hidden hinge pins. To drill the ends of the lid for the hinge pins to fit, use the procedures described in chapter seven, and then rout the inside back edge with a ¼" roundover bit to clear for opening the lid. Drilling the hinge-pin holes in the ends follows the same procedures used in making the checkerboard inlay box, except that you determine the locations for the hinge holes differently. First set up the top-to-bottom distance, allowing ¹⁄₃₂" for clearance in opening, and index the position of the hole from the top edge of the box. To determine the location for stop-blocks to further position the holes, place the back piece in the mortise provided for it, and with a steel rule, follow the angle of the back, marking a line on the end piece to indicate the location of the back edge of the top after assembly. Measure the space between the holes in the ends of the lid and the back edge of the lid using the dial caliper. Use that distance to mark a line on the ends, measuring from the line of the angle of the back. This gives the outside position of the hole for the hinge pin to fit the lid. It is necessary to adjust the angle of the drill press table to compensate for the angle of the ends, or to use a matching piece with the same angle, reversed, to hold the end piece in proper relation to the drill. This simpler approach requires less setup time and leaves the table at 90° for other uses. Once you have set up to drill one end accurately, it is easy to set up for the opposite end using the technique shown right.

## Shape the Lid

Use the jig on the band saw that you used to cut the radius in the bracelet box top (chapter five) to first give the lid a curved shape. Then alter the shape by sculpting it on the stationary belt sander. This is not a precise operation. It helps to adjust the belt sander to a comfortable working height and to get a good secure body stance before starting. This is a risky operation in that a small slip can give unintended results. A comfortable body position is the first step in reducing that risk.

**3** Drill for the hinge pins; use a matching piece to level the workpiece with the drill press. The stop block helps to accurately index for drilling the opposite end as shown in the next photos.

**4** Now drill the holes in the opposite ends.

**5**

Drill a piece of scrap wood clear through, and then turn it over and use it to set up the stop-block for drilling the opposite end of the box.

**7**

Shape the sculpted top on the belt sander.

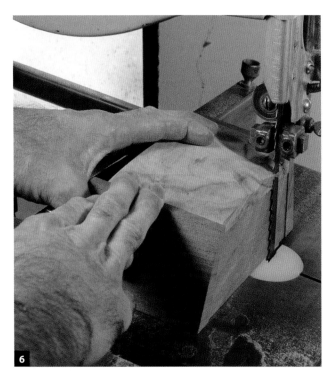

**6**

Use the band saw with the table tilted to match the angles of the sides to trim the box ends and lid.

## Dry-Assemble the Box

First assemble the box without glue, allowing you to sand the front and back edges prior to fitting the walnut pull on the lid. Use the band saw, set at the same angle as the sides, to cut the end pieces and lid roughly to shape. Next, sand the surfaces flush on the stationary belt sander.

## Attach the Pull

Attach an angled fence to the fence on the router table to hold the box lid at the correct angle to the ⅛" straight cutter, and use stop-blocks to control the length of cut. Adjust the depth of cut of the router table to be just a tiny bit deeper than the tenon on the end of the pull to allow for finish sanding and gluing.

## MAKING THE SECRET DRAWER

This box is a production item in my shop, and I keep the drawer simple so that the drawers in the many boxes I

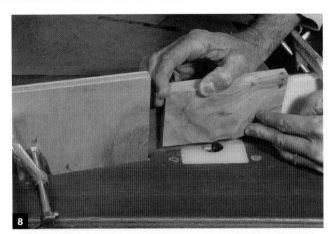

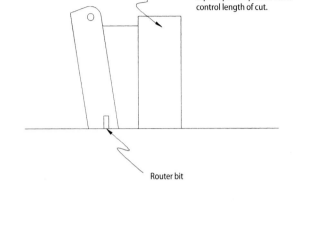

Fence

Routing for lid pull on angled top. Stops clamped on fence control length of cut.

Router bit

**8** Pull the trial-assembled box apart, and with an angled guide piece clamped to the router table fence, set up stops and rout the front edge of the lid with a ⅛" straight-cut bit for the small walnut pull to fit.

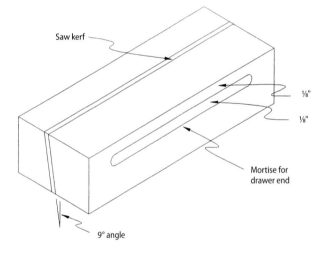

Saw kerf

⅛"

⅛"

Mortise for drawer end

9° angle

**9** Form the drawer by gluing parts to the Baltic birch plywood drawer bottom; use brads to give added strength.

make will work smoothly without a lot of fooling around. The drawer bottom serves double duty by acting as drawer guides. The drawer sides are glued and nailed to the drawer bottom, and the drawer front is made of the same walnut as the ends for color and grain match.

## Make the Drawer Face

To make the drawer face, cut a piece of walnut to match the angle of the sides by resawing the piece into angled strips. Cut the angled strips to the same length as the box ends. With the ⅛" straight-cut bit in the router, cut the mortise for the box bottom to fit using the same technique as in making the ends. Use the drawer guide

slots cut in the front and back of the box to determine the position of the fence. Index this cut from the top edge of the drawer front, and make an extra for the inevitable trial and error involved in getting a good fit.

## Make the Drawer Sides

Resaw sugar maple and plane it to size. Then, using the mitered cutoff table on the table saw, cut mitered corners on the parts. Cut the drawer back to exact size and leave the sides long to be cut to equal length using the 90° cutoff table on the table saw, with a stop-block to be certain they are uniform in length.

Assemble the box permanently with glue spread in the mortises. If the mortises and tenons fit perfectly, the box assembles without clamps. If necessary, use clamps and angled cushion blocks to hold the joints tight for gluing.

Begin forming the tenon on the walnut lift tab with a straight-cut router bit. The open space between the fence and bit determines the height of the lift tab.

## Assemble the Drawers

Make a jig to hold the side pieces in place while the bottom is glued and nailed in place with slight-headed brads. To assemble the drawer, first glue the box bottom in the mortise cut in the drawer front; lay the side and back pieces in the jig, squeeze a line of glue on the pieces, align the drawer bottom in place and then tack brads into place. After the glue has dried, drill a ⅛" hole through the center of the drawer back for the stop pin, which will be tacked into place when the box is completely finished.

# FINAL ASSEMBLY AND FINISHING

## Assemble the Box

Follow the same assembly procedures used in assembling the checkerboard inlay box (chapter seven).

## Check for Square

Check to see that the box is square by opening and closing the lid and observing its fit. If necessary, clamp the box together, using cushion blocks cut at the same angle as the sides and fronts to provide even clamping pressure.

## Sand the Box

With the drawer in place, sand the box on the stationary belt sander, starting out with #100-grit to sand the ends even with the sides and the drawer facing even with the end, and to sand the top edges of the ends even with contours of the lid. Then change belts to #150-grit, and repeat the sanding operation. Use the inverted orbital sander to sand the box through grits #180, #240 and #320.

## Finish the Box

Apply the Danish oil finish to the box, with the drawer removed. I do two coats the first day, waiting about 30 minutes between coats and about an hour before rubbing out the finish with a clean, soft cloth. After about 24 hours, I apply a third coat, which I rub out when the surface starts to feel a little sticky. When the finish is completely dry, I tack a ⅛" dowel pin in the hole in the drawer to serve as a drawer stop.

# MAKING YOUR OWN BOX PULLS

The very small lift tabs can be made easily and safely despite their small size. In making small parts, I like to do all the important steps while they are in a large enough form to be manageable.

## Size the Pull Stock

Start by resawing a piece of walnut to about ¼" thick and with the tapered sanding disc in the table saw, sand it down to about ³⁄₁₆" thick. Set up the router table with a ⁵⁄₁₆" straight cutter and make a cut on each side, about ¹⁄₃₂" deep, leaving ⅛" at the center. Position the fence so that the lift tab will be about ⅛" high.

# CHAPTER NINE

# TEA CHEST

I made my first tea box for a friend's fine restaurant. It was inlaid with burled walnut and curly maple cows grazing on a field of Ozark Mountain cherry. Sometimes we are drawn to a project by the challenges it offers, and then discover that even though we are successful in a project, the work itself does not continue to interest us. That kind of sums up my relationship with the type of inlay known as marquetry. Because I have done a lot of inlay over the years, I am often asked to do this type of work. It is important for us, as woodworkers, to discover the kinds of work that we most enjoy and to follow the path that our pleasure outlines for us. From the inlay patterns I have developed and the boxes I have designed, you can see that I am most drawn to simple and elegant lines. I am most at home letting the wood do the talking. I think of the phrase "working with wood" as describing a partnership agreement. The important word in the phrase is *with*. The craftsman and the wood contribute equally to the finished piece.

This tea chest is made from a very special and prized piece of crotch-figured walnut (from the intersection of tree limbs) and a very simple inlay of fiddleback maple and cherry. This box is made with the box joint (from the days of finely crafted cigar boxes). In those days, cigar boxes with this joint were described as having "locked" corners, and were associated with quality cigars – cigars worth going to greater expense to package. This joint is now more commonly known as the finger joint. I use a jig on the router table to cut the fingers and hollows for the box joint but, because I want inlay on the top edges, the final fingers are mitered on the table saw. This allows me to complete the inlaying of the box before it is assembled. I use a solid carbide spiral-end mill bit in the router to get a very clean cut. I designed the tea chest to hold various packaged teas in nine compartments. The size and shape of the compartments, and the overall shape and size of the box are determined by the packaging of the various teas.

## MATERIALS LIST

| 5/4 Black walnut | (for the front, back and sides) |
| --- | --- |
| Crotch-figured black walnut | ¾" (for top) |
| 4/4 black walnut | (to resaw for dividers) |
| Birch plywood | ¼" (for the bottom) |

## BUILDING THE BOX

### Resaw the Box Sides

Use black walnut for the sides, and resaw on the band saw from 5/4 stock. This allows you to form nearly perfect grain patterns around the perimeter of the box, with one resawn piece forming the front and right side, and the matching piece forming the back and left side.

Plane the resawn stock to ⁷⁄₁₆" thick before cutting it to the dimensions for the box.

### Make a Jig for Locked Corners

To make the jig to cut the locked corners, take a piece of ¾" birch veneer plywood about 12" x 24", and make two dado cuts in it about ¼" deep by ¾" wide, about 2" in from each edge. This provides a track for the upper part to slide over the router bit. Cut this into two pieces: The one that forms the top of the jig is about 8" long; the other longer one forms the base for attaching the router. Cut a second ¼" x ¾" dado about 4" in from the edge of the upper jig part and 90° to and on the opposite side of the first dados. In this dado attach a fence to hold the stock, and install screws from underneath to hold the fence in position. Attach runners in the dados

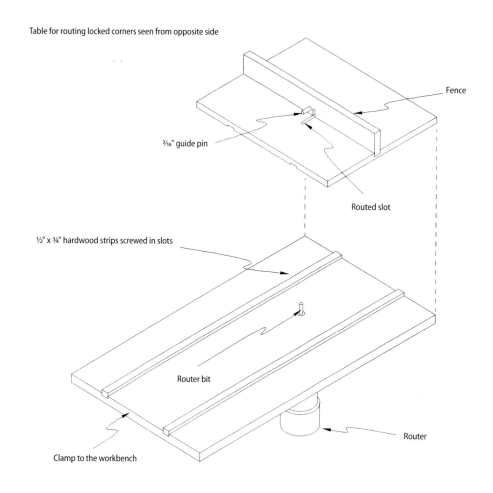

Table for routing locked corners seen from opposite side

Fence

³⁄₁₆" guide pin

Routed slot

½" x ¾" hardwood strips screwed in slots

Router bit

Router

Clamp to the workbench

1

Use a router table and spiral cutter to make the locked corners of the tea chest. The 3/16" brass pin from brass welding rod stock matches the diameter of the spiral cutter. Make the cuts, holding the front and back pieces against the fence and brass pin, lifting each piece over the pin for consecutive cuts.

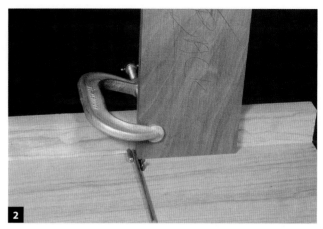

2

Clamp the matching sides to the fence for the first cut, using an additional piece of brass rod for a spacer.

3

After the first cut is made, additional cuts follow the same proceedure as for the front and back. To allow for the mitered corner, stop your cuts one cut short of the width of the side.

of the base part of the jig, about 1/2" x 3/4", so that it fits into the dados of the upper and lower parts. Use screws to attach these runners to the base section and machine screws to attach the router base to the underside of the lower unit. With a plunge-cutting bit in the router, and the lower unit clamped firmly to the workbench, turn on the router and gradually raise the cut until it passes up through the lower unit. Then repeat the procedure with a larger straight-cut router bit to cut the hole large enough for the collet of the router to enter the space, bringing the router bit closer to the workpiece. Then, with the bit to cut the locked corners in the router, put the upper part or the jig on the tracks and position it so that the router bit will, when raised, cut into the area just slightly ahead of the fence. Make the cuts in small increments, raising the bit a hair and sliding the upper part of the jig back and forth. Repeat this until the bit comes up through the surface with enough height to cut the length of the fingers required. I used a 3/16" brass pin as a guide pin to match the 3/16" carbide cutter used. To install the guide pin, I drilled a hole in the fence, about 3/8" from the bottom edge, so that it would be just high enough when installed in the jig to keep from collecting sawdust. With the guide pin in place, I cut test pieces to check the placement of the guide pin. If the fingers are too loose, I loosen the screws attaching the fence to the platform and nudge the fence slightly away from the cutter. Then I drill for a new screw in a new location to

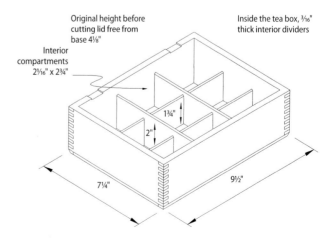

Original height before cutting lid free from base 4 1/8"

Inside the tea box, 3/16" thick interior dividers

Interior compartments 2 1/16" x 2 3/4"

1 3/4"

2"

7 1/4"

9 1/2"

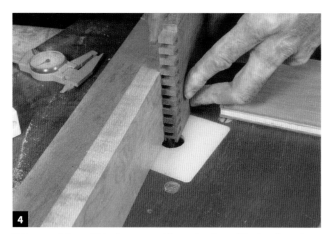

4

Using a straight-cut bit in the router table, cut the channel for the inlay to fit. The inlay is made of fiddleback maple banded in cherry.

5

With the tapered sanding disc tilted to 90° in the table saw, sand the inlay flush with the top edges of the walnut sides.

hold the fence in position. If the fingers are too tight, I nudge the fence slightly toward the cutter.

## Cut the Fingers

Index all the cuts from the bottom edge, cutting the sides first, and then the fronts and backs. In cutting the sides, start with the bottom edges up against the guide pin, and hold the workpiece tight against the fence while sliding the platform forward and back across the router bit. Position subsequent cuts by lifting the finished finger over the guide pin. On the side pieces, stop short of cutting all the fingers, leaving the last ones to be cut into a miter joint at the top. To cut the fingers for the fronts and backs, use a shim between the guide pin and the first finger while you use a C-clamp to hold it firmly to the fence. This is to make the fingers of the fronts and backs fit the sides. Remove the shim before making the cut.

## Make the Inlay for the Top

Inlay the top edges of the tea chest before the mitered corners are cut. The inlay is very simple, with a 3/16"-wide strip of fiddleback maple laminated between two thin strips of cherry. Cut the cherry strips about 3/32" thick from 3/4" cherry stock, and glue them to the fiddleback maple, with blocks of solid wood on both sides to evenly distribute clamping pressure. After the glue has dried, joint one edge flush on the jointer. To bring the strips down to a uniform thickness of 5/16", use

6

Use the miter cutoff box on the table saw to cut the miters at the box corners. Rather than take time to change to a dado blade for the miters on the sides, I lower the blade to cut only what is neccessary for the corner to fit, and make several passes to cut away the waste.

7

The first cut to shape the edges of the top panel establishes the tongue depth.

The second cut defines the tongue length.

This final cut, with the blade set at 8°, establishes the shape of the panel.

With the start and stop points penciled on the router table fence, rout the front, back and sides for the top panel and bottom to fit. Cut a test piece to check the position of the cut so that the bevel on the top comes out even with the beveled sides.

the tapered sanding disc in the table saw. This disc is used in place of a blade, and because the disc is tapered, it allows stock to be fed into it along the fence, with the abrasives cutting deeper as the stock moves toward the center of the disc. Because of the taper, the blade must be adjusted a bit off 90° to uniformly cut the strip top to bottom. Cut a bit from each side of the strip until the cherry bands are each about 1/16" thick and, more importantly, the total width of the stock is 5/16" to match the width of the cutter for routing the inlay channel. Cut the inlay strips from this stock at about 1/8" thick to allow for the angle that will form in the top edges of the box parts.

## Install the Inlay

To rout for the inlay, use a 5/16" straight-cut router bit. Position the cutter to center the inlay in the stock, leaving about 1/16" of walnut on each side of the channel. Cut the inlay in lengths just barely over the lengths of the box parts, and glue them in place using blocking against the inlay to provide even clamping pressure.

## Sand the Inlay Flush

After the glue has dried, use the tapered sanding disc to sand the inlay flush with the surrounding walnut so you will have a good square surface to cut the miters in the corners.

## Miter the Side Pieces

Use the miter cutoff box to cut the corners on the sides, front and back. On the front and back pieces cut the miters clear through the top fingers, but on the side pieces lower the blade so that it cuts just enough away to allow the side to give clearance for the mitered finger to fit. Because the saw blade I use leaves a V-cut, when cutting the sides to match, I lower the blade just enough to allow a small cleanup cut with a straight chisel.

## Shape the Edges

Shape the top edges of the sides, front and back of the tea chest using the tapered sanding blade in the table saw. The object here is to provide a smooth transition into the angles that will be formed in the top panel. Check the ends of the parts to make sure you don't come close to sanding through the inlay.

**11**

With a straight-cut bit in the router table, size the ¼" plywood bottom panel to fit the ³⁄₁₆" dados in the front, back and sides.

**12**

To rout for the dividers, first rout the mortise in the sides. Stop blocks ensure the mortise lengths will be the same for each piece.

## Cut the Top Panel

Assemble the box to get the finished dimensions for the top panel, adding ⅜" each direction to allow for the ³⁄₁₆" x ³⁄₁₆" tongues on the top panel, and subtracting ³⁄₃₂" from the width for possible expansion and ¹⁄₃₂" from the length to ease assembly. Cut the tongues on the panel and shape the top.

## Rout Dados for the Top and Bottom

Use the router table and a ³⁄₁₆" router bit to rout for the top and bottom to fit. To avoid difficulties in assembling the box, plan the dado to house the top to correlate with the opening between fingers on the front and back. This will allow the top to slide in place after most of the interior elements of the box are in place during assembly. In order for the ¼" birch plywood bottom to fit the ³⁄₁₆" dado, use a straight-cut router bit and rout the piece to fit.

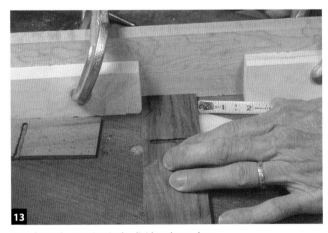

**13**

Next, I rout the mortises in the dividers themselves.

## Make the Interior Dividers

Make the interior dividers from ¾" black walnut stock, resawn, planed and then sanded to ³⁄₁₆" thick, using the tapered sanding disc. In order for the stock to fit into the rounded mortises, I rout the top edges with a ⅛" roundover bit. Note that the dividers running from front to back are taller than the side to side ones and require longer mortises. The procedure for setting up and routing for the dividers is shown right.

**14**

The routed mortises in the dividers.

**15**

Routing a roundover on the top edge allows the dividers to fit the channels routed for them. Standing the pieces on edge keeps the pilot bearing in contact with the flat surface.

**16**

Use spacer blocks, cut to the dimensions of the interior compartments, to hold the dividers in position during assembly.

## Sanding

Before assembling the tea chest, sand all the interior parts, the inside surfaces of the sides, front and back, the inside and outside of the top panel, both sides of the bottom and the inlaid edges. Use a sanding block to sand the inside edges where the sides, front and back will intersect the top panel, and also the panel edges where they intersect the front, back and sides. This will visually soften the junction between these parts and give them more definition.

## Assemble the Chest

Assemble the tea chest as a single unit, planning to cut the lid from the base after it is all glued together. An advantage of this method is that the top and bottom will align perfectly with each other. The disadvantage is that the interior parts can make assembly of a closed space challenging. Use blocks cut to size to hold the interior parts in place during assembly. To make the parts slip together easily, sharpen the interior parts slightly on the 6" x 48" belt sander.

## Cut the Top From the Bottom

Use the table saw, with the blade raised just slightly above the 7/16" thickness of the sides to make the cuts separating the top from the bottom. Because of the shape of the top, run the bottom of the box along the fence. After each cut, replace the saw-kerf with a shim

**17**

Slide the top into place, and then the end, with glue spread on the matching fingers of the joint.

As you make the cuts separating the top from the bottom, replace the saw-kerf with shims and hold the box together with tape.

Use the router and straight-cut bit to rout away most of the waste from the hinge mortise, leaving just a bit to clean up with the chisel.

to hold the top and bottom in proper relation to each other and to prevent a miscut.

## Clean Up the Cut

If the blade cuts well, and the fence is perfectly parallel to it, you may not need this step. Otherwise, clean up the saw cuts and make them even with a handplane.

## Install the Hinges

To assemble the box, use hinges that open only to 95°, eliminating the need for a lid support. Use a router to remove most of the waste from the hinge mortises. Carefully mark the location for the hinges on the back edge of the top and bottom to make certain they are in perfect alignment. By using the router, you are able to get an accurate depth for the hinge mortises and better control of the tolerances between the lid and base of the box.

## Install the Finger Pull

Use a small finger pull on the lid of the box to make it easy to open. I used the same pull, slightly shortened, on the sculpted pecan box in chapter eight.

## Shape the Sides of the Box

Use a handplane to cut a very small chamfer on the outside edges of the top, and on the edges of the top and bottom where they intersect. Use the chamfering bit in the router table to rout a slightly larger chamfer around the bottom edge, making it a bit more elegant and easier to pick up.

## Finishing Up

I added small brass feet, which are glued in ⁵⁄₁₆" holes in the corners, after sanding and applying the oil finish. The hardness of the crotch walnut panel enables it to take a tremendous finish that invites the touch.

# CHAPTER TEN

# JEWELRY BOX WITH HAND-CUT DOVETAILS

Nothing expresses a craftsman's interest in quality as well as dovetails. To cut them by hand is a challenge for beginning woodworkers, offering satisfaction and self-confidence in reward. On this jewelry chest, I use a mitered dovetail on the top edge, which allows the use of a simple inlaid banding. Simple work, with emphasis on detail, can give a piece lasting value. The sycamore used for inlay in the box is quartersawn, revealing its beautiful, soft, iridescent patterning. I use a great deal of cherry in the various pieces of furniture that I make, and the cherry parts for this box are leftovers and cutoff from a dining set. The dimensions of the box were determined in part by the size of the cherry panel I've used in the top.

# MATERIALS LIST

| | | |
|---|---|---|
| Cherry | | ⅝" (for sides, front, back and drawer front) |
| | | ¾" (for top) |
| | | ¾" (resawn to ⁵⁄₁₆" for the sliding compartments) |
| Cherry veneer plywood | | ¼" (for bottom) |
| Baltic birch plywood sliding compartment | | ⅛" (for drawer and tray bottoms) |
| 4/4 cherry | | (to resaw for drawer sides) |
| Side | 2 pcs. | ⅝" x 5⅜" x 10¹⁄₁₆" |
| Back | 1 pc. | ⅝" x 5⅜" x 12¹⁄₁₆" |
| Front | 1 pc. | ⅝" x 3¾" x 12¹⁄₁₆" |
| Top fill strips | 2 pcs. | ⅜" x ⅝" x 10¹³⁄₁₆" |
| | 2 pcs. | ⅜" x ⅝" x 8¹³⁄₁₆" |
| Top panel | 1 pc. | ¾" x 10½" 8⅜" |
| Box bottom | 1 pc. | 11⅛" x 9¹⁄₁₆" x ¼" |
| Tray slides | 2 pcs. | ³⁄₁₆" x ¼" x 10¾" |
| Drawer guides | 2 pcs. | ³⁄₁₆" x ¼" x 8⅞" |
| Box dividers | 2 pcs. | ³⁄₁₆" x 1" x 9¹⁄₁₆" |

### Drawer parts

| | | |
|---|---|---|
| Front* | 1 pc. | ⅝" x 1⅝" x 12¹⁄₁₆" |
| Sides | 2 pcs. | ⅜" x 1⅝" x 8¹⁵⁄₁₆" |
| Bottom | 2 pcs. | ³⁄₁₆" x 1" x 9¹⁄₁₆" |

### Tray parts

| | | |
|---|---|---|
| Sides | 4 pcs. | ⁵⁄₁₆" x 1⅜" x 8¼" |
| Ends | 4 pcs. | ⁵⁄₁₆" x 1⅜" x 3⅝" |
| Dividers | 6 pcs. | ⅛" x 1" x 3¼" |
| Bottoms | 2 pcs. | ⅛" x 3¼" x 8¼" |

*Cut drawer front from same piece as box front

# TOOLS LIST

| |
|---|
| Table saw |
| 45° chamfering bit |
| Band saw |
| Planer |
| Router table |
| Dozuki (Japanese backsaw) |
| Marking gauge |
| ⅜" and ¼" chisels |
| ³⁄₁₆" and ½" straight-cut router bits |
| Sliding T-bevel |
| Chip-carving knife |

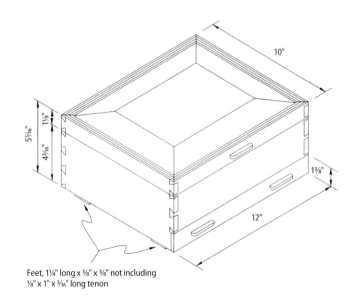

Feet, 1¼" long x ⅜" x ⅜" not including
⅛" x 1" x ³⁄₁₆" long tenon

Use a marking gauge set about ⅟₃₂" over the thickness of the stock, a sliding T-bevel at a 1:8 ratio and a small square and pencil to lay out the dovetails, using the square to continue the markings around the corners.

Use the dozuki saw to cut the tails, following the pencil lines to where they intersect the line from the marking gauge, except for the tails in the top corners of the stock.

To cut the mitered dovetails for the top corners, follow the cut line on the inside, taking care not to cut through to the other side.

# MAKING HAND-CUT DOVETAILS

## Lay Out Pins

Start this project by laying out the dovetails. Use a marking gauge to transfer the thickness of each cherry piece to the piece it will be joined with. Then use the sliding bevel, with the angle adjusted to an 8:1 ratio (the preferred angle for hardwood dovetails), to mark the tails on the side pieces. Lay out the dovetails, remembering to allow for the saw-kerf when the top is cut away from the base of the box. Then use a chip-carving knife and a square to mark cut lines around the ends of the side stock.

## Cut Out the Pins

Use the dozuki to follow your cut lines. A special feature of this box is the mitered dovetail used in the corners, which allows for the continuous inlay band around the perimeter of the top.

## Allow for the Top Miter

Use the dozuki to help make the miter cut by cutting in only on the inside of the top corners.

## Remove the Waste Between the Tails

Using the band saw, reduce chiseling time by removing some waste between the tails.

Use the mitered cutoff box on the table saw to cut the miter on the top corner of the sides with the blade cutting a bit shy of the dozuki saw cut, leaving a little cleanup work for the chisel.

**5**

With a quick cut with a straight chisel, finish forming the mitered tail.

**6**

Lay the box side in position on the box back to mark it for cutting the pins. Use a knife to scribe the cut line, and then a small square to continue the cut lines down the face of the stock to meet the marking gauge line.

## Clean Up the Tails

Now you can use the ¾" straight chisel to clean up your dozuki saw cuts, and the ⅜" straight chisel to remove the remaining stock between the tails. To finish the mitered dovetail at the corner, use the cutoff box on the table saw, with the blade raised almost to the height of the dovetail, allowing a small cleanup allowance for the chisel.

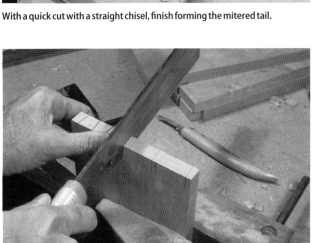

**7**

Use the dozuki saw again to follow the cut lines, being careful that the saw follows along the tail side of the pins.

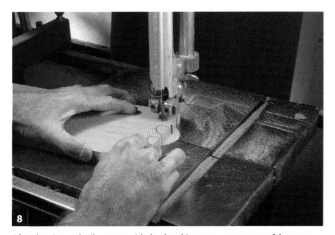

**8**

After the pins and tails are cut with the dozuki saw, cut away some of the waste between the pins by using the band saw. With the workpiece face down, you can better avoid cutting into the pins by mistake. This step will speed up the cutting of the dovetails. Plus, by making the work easier, they will come out cleaner.

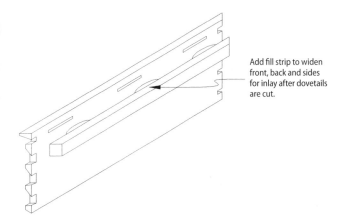

Add fill strip to widen front, back and sides for inlay after dovetails are cut.

9
With straight chisels, remove the rest of the waste, cutting along the marking gauge line from both sides of the stock. Clean up the pins and adjust them as necessary to fit the dovetails.

## Lay Out the Pins
To cut the pins, position the tails so that you can use the knife to mark them directly where they will fit between the pins. Use the square to continue the marks down the sides of the stock for the front and back.

## Cut Out the Pins
Use the dozuki again to follow the cut lines, being careful that the saw follows along the tail side of the pins.

## Cut Away the Waste Between Pins
Cut away some of the waste between the pins using the band saw. Make two cuts straight into the pin area, as shown, and then two cuts at an angle to cut away the waste. Use a straight chisel to finish cutting the pins.

## Miter the Top Pins
Before cleaning up the pins and tails to fit, use the mitered cutoff box on the table saw to cut the top pins on the front and back pieces to fit the mitered tails on the sides.

## Clean Up the Sides and Fit
Clean up the pins and tails, adjusting them as necessary to fit. Then, when the box is pushed together for a test fitting, pry the box apart a little bit, take the dozuki and cut lightly into the miter. This cleans it up and gives a tight fit when the box is glued up.

10
After cutting the mitered top corners of the front and back on the table saw, assemble the box for a test fit. With the joints open slightly, use the dozuki saw to cut into the miters. Be careful not to cut into the dovetail itself. When the joints are pushed closed, the two sides of the miter will close to a perfect fit.

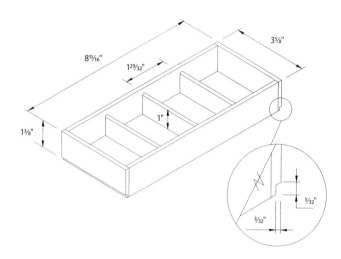

Use the router table with fence, stop-blocks and 3/16" carbide spiral cutter to rout for the bottom, sliding tray guides and dividers to fit in the front and back pieces, and for the bottom and drawer guides to fit in the sides. Use the router table to rout channels in the drawer sides to fit the drawer guides.

## INLAYING THE TOP

### Cut Strips for the Top

After the dovetails are cut and fitted, cut strips of cherry to attach to the insides of the front, back and sides to broaden the area available for inlaying. Miter these just a little bit oversize in length, and use #0 size biscuits to attach them to the inside top edges of the box parts. Before gluing these parts in place, chamfer the bottom edge and sand the parts. This will be difficult once these pieces are glued in place. When gluing them in place be careful that the ends extend just barely beyond the edges of the mitered dovetails. This will allow you to trim them off again with the dozuki after the inlay is in place.

### Make the Inlay

To make the inlay, follow the procedure used for making the inlay for the tea chest in chapter nine, except plane the sycamore to ½" in thickness and resaw the walnut banding to about 3/32", so that the finished banding will be about 5/8" in dimension to better fit the proportions of this larger box. Before shaping and inlaying the top edge of the box, use the table saw to cut the top parts away from the bottom, unlike the technique used in making the tea chest, which was assembled before the top was cut away. This makes dadoing the top edge for the raised panel, shaping the top angle of the lid pieces and inlaying

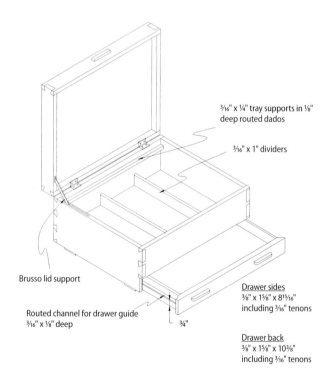

3/16" x 1/4" tray supports in 1/8" deep routed dados

3/16" x 1" dividers

Brusso lid support

Routed channel for drawer guide
3/16" x 1/8" deep

3/4"

Drawer sides
3/8" x 1 5/8" x 8 15/16"
including 3/16" tenons

Drawer back
3/8" x 1 5/8" x 10 3/8"
including 3/16" tenons

12

Assemble the box with glue spread on the pins and tails.

13

After inlaying is complete, use the dozuki saw again to cut into the miter with the joint open just a bit. It is good to make sure that the frame is square as you do this to get a good fit.

## Make the Drawer and Trays

Make the bottom drawer using a mortise-and-tenon joint to connect the sides to the front and back and use ⅛" Baltic birch for the drawer bottom. Fit the drawer sides to the drawer guides using the 3⁄16" end mill in the router. Index the cut from the bottom edge of the drawer side so that the bottom edge of the drawer will be flush with the bottom edge of the box, and a tight fit can be adjusted by trimming the top edge of the drawer. To make sure that the drawer moves freely on the guide, adjust the fence slightly to widen the cut with a second pass. Make the trays using the mortise-and-tenon technique shown in chapter six. The technique for making the dividers is shown in chapter nine.

## Cut the Drawer Opening

Before assembly, cut away the areas on the sides where the drawer will fit, and cut the chamfer to fit the shape of the drawer. Trim the bottom panel to fit into the 3⁄16" dado, and sand all the inside surfaces of the box.

them easier operations. Unlike inlaying the tea chest, cut the angle in the top edge first, and then inlay it using the router table techniques described earlier in the book.

## INSTALLING DRAWERS AND DIVIDERS

### Cut Dados and Mortises in the Sides and Top

Before the box is assembled, perform several routing operations to provide for drawer guide strips in the sides, top compartment slide strips in the front and back, mortises for compartment dividers in the front and back, and a 3⁄16" dado in the front, back and sides for the interior panel of the box. Use the 3⁄16" carbide spiral end mill for all of these operations, changing the fence settings and arrangement of stop-blocks as needed.

## ASSEMBLE THE BOX

### Glue Up the Sides

Next, put the front and back together around the interior dividers, spread glue on the pins and tails and push the sides into place. Use bar clamps to pull the sides in tight, checking with a tape measure to make sure the box is square.

## Assemble the Top

Before assembling the top, put it together for a trial assembly and use the dozuki to recut the corners, trimming the inlaid corners to match. As before, spread the joint just a bit, the width of a saw-kerf, and cut down into the joint, being careful not to cut into the dovetail. Rather than overcut, you can stop short of cutting too far, pull the joint back apart and finish the cut with a straight chisel. Make the raised panel top using the same techniques used to make the top for the tea chest, and sand it on the inside before assembly. Cut the dado for the panel to fit in the top with the table saw and a ¼" dado blade. Position the cut so that the angled surfaces of the top panel will meet the angled edge of the dovetailed frame. In assembling the top, put a bit of glue in the dado at the center of the sides of the top to keep the panel centered in the frame, while leaving it free to expand and contract as needed, and apply glue to the pins and dovetails as in assembling the base. To check the square of the lid, place it on the base and feel to see that it lines up flush on all sides.

## FINISHING THE BOX

To complete the jewelry box, sand the outside, chamfer the edges very slightly where the top meets the bottom, and chamfer the bottom edges of the box and the drawer front. Assemble the drawer. After the sliding compartments are made, make a rabbet cut on each end so that it will fit over the guides and slide smoothly without touching either the inside of the box or the sliding-tray ends. Make little walnut feet, tenoned to fit in mortises routed in the bottom of the box after assembly, to lift it slightly above the table and walnut pulls as described previously.

Use drawn brass hinges, which you can install using the same technique described in making the tea chest, and a lid support from Woodcraft Supply on this project. Use the plunge router to rout the mortise for the lid support, and a ¼" brad-point drill bit to drill in the top for the other end to fit.

**14**

To assemble the top, spread glue on the pins and tail and just a small dab only at the center of the dado where the panel fits. This is to keep the panel centered in the lid during changes in humidity.

# CHAPTER ELEVEN

# EARRING & PIN CHEST

M any times, the designs used in my work have evolved from other projects. A number of years ago I made a cabinet for a friend to give to his wife for keeping and displaying her collection of pins. The cabinet was a free-form design, with dinosaur heads and parts attached in a sliding dovetail track enabling them to be rearranged like a puzzle. I used the fabric wings for the first time in that piece: They are an excellent way to display and store fine jewelry without it being bunched in drawers where they can be nicked and scratched, more worn-out than worn out. This cabinet is designed to hold countless pairs of earrings and pins. Brass pins installed in the doors allow necklaces to also be hung. The drawer at the base provides conventional storage for larger items.

# MATERIALS LIST

| | | |
|---|---|---|
| Ash | | $^{13}/_{16}$" |
| Black walnut | | 1" x 1" x 20"<br>*(for raised inlay)* |
| Tops and bottoms | 4 pcs. | ¾" x 1⅝" x 11⅛" |
| | 4 pcs. | ¾" x 1⅝" x 8⅛" |
| Vertical stretchers | 3 pcs. | ¾" x 1⅜" x 12¹/₁₆" |
| Back panel | 1 pc. | ⅛" x 6⅛" x 12⁹/₁₆" |
| Base and drawer front | 2 pcs. | ¾" x 1¹⁵/₁₆" x 11⅛" |
| | 2 pcs. | ¾" x 1¹⁵/₁₆" x 8⅛"¹ |
| Interior wing supports | 7 pcs. | ⅝" x ¾" x 11¹⁵/₁₆" |
| | 8 pcs. | ⁵/₁₆" x 1" x 4³/₁₆"¹ |
| | 4 pcs. | ⁵/₁₆" x 1" x 3⁵/₁₆" |
| | 2 pcs. | ⁵/₁₆" x 1" x 4⅞" |

**Door parts**

| | | |
|---|---|---|
| Stiles | 2 pcs. | ¾" 1½" x 12" |
| | 2 pcs. | ¾" x 1¼" x 12" |
| Rails | 2 pcs. | ¾" x 1½" x 10½"² |
| | 2 pcs. | ¾" x 1¾" x 10½"² |
| | 2 pcs. | ¾" x 1½" x 4⅛"¹³ |
| | 2 pcs. | ¾" x 1½" x 6¼"¹³ |
| | 2 pcs. | ¾" x 1¾" x 4⅛"¹³ |
| | 2 pcs. | ¾" x 1¾" x 6¼"¹³ |
| Panels | 2 pcs. | ¼" x 3¹⁷/₃₂" x 9¼"⁴ |
| | 2 pcs. | ¼" 5¹¹/₁₆" x 9¼"⁴ |
| Tabs | 2 pcs. | ¼" x 1¼" x ⁵/₁₆" |
| Corner blocks | 4 pcs. | ¼" x 1¼" x 1¾" |

**Drawer Parts**

| | | |
|---|---|---|
| Sides | 2 pcs. | ⁵/₁₆" x 1¹⁵/₁₆" x 6⅞" |
| Back | 1 pc. | ⁵/₁₆" x 1¹⁵/₁₆" x 9⅜" |
| Bottom | 1 pc. | ⅛" x 6⅝" 9¼"⁵ |
| Pulls | 2 pcs. | ⁵/₁₆" x 1¼" x ⁹/₁₆"⁵ |
| Hardware | | |
| Brainerd hinges<br>*(open, with magnetic catches and catch plates)* | 2 pcs. | ⁵/₁₆" x 1" x ¹³/₁₆" |
| Brass pins | 16 pcs. | ⅛" x ⅝"<br>*(for necklace hangers)* |
| | 14 pcs. | ³/₁₆" x ¾"<br>*(pivot pins for wings)* |

¹ Length includes ½" tenons.
² Measurement before cutting miter joints.
³ Measurement after cutting miter joints. Length includes ¾" tenons.
⁴ Finished dimension before gluing miter joint.
⁵ Length includes tenons.

# TOOLS LIST

| |
|---|
| Planer |
| Plunge router |
| Jointer |
| ⅜" and ¼" carbide spiral cutter |
| Router table |
| ¼" straight-cut bit |
| 45° chamfering bit |
| ⅛" slotting cutter |
| Table saw |

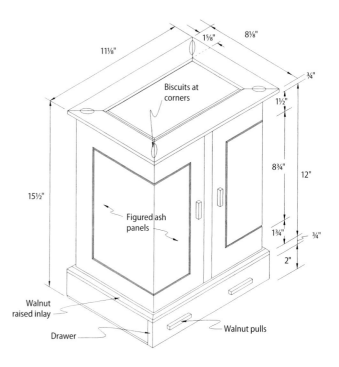

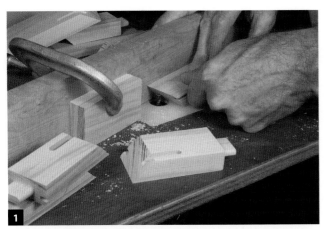

Use the router table, ¼" straight-cut bit, fence and stop-blocks to cut slots for corner braces for the doors. Reposition the stop-blocks to rout the matching parts.

Use the miter cutoff box on the table saw to cut the five-sided corner blocks.

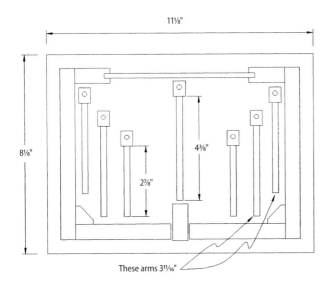

11⅛"

8⅛"

4⅜"

2⅞"

These arms 3¹¹⁄₁₆"

## MAKING THE CABINET

### Prepare the Stock for the Doors

I start by resawing the door panels on the band saw, but because my band saw has only a 6" depth of cut, I cut the panels in two sections, each just a little wider than needed to form the L-shaped panels. Plane these panels to ¼" thick. Next, cut the frame parts to size and cut the stiles to length, but leave the rails long so that they can be cut for the mitered corner.

### Cut Mortises and Dados for the Doors

Use the plunge router to cut the mortises in the stiles, and then cut the tenons on the rails. Next, use the ⅛" slotting cutter to cut the dados for the door panels to fit, cutting from end to end on the rails but cutting only between the mortises on the stiles. Set the slotting cutter height so that the finished panels will be flush with the outside surface of the stiles and rails.

### Cut the Door Panels to Size

Cut the panel parts to length and cut tongues on three sides, leaving the edges where the panel parts will be glued together alone. Use a V-groove bit to chamfer the panel edge where it will intersect the stiles and rails.

### Dry-Assemble the Doors

Assemble the stiles and rails without glue so they can be pulled apart later, and use a 45° chamfering bit to chamfer the inside edges to match the panels. Use a straight chisel to cut into the corners, finishing the cut. Tilt the arbor of the saw to 45° to cut the rails to length, mitering them to fit back together to form the L-shaped doors, and while the saw is still at 45°, cut the miters in the panels, allowing just a little space for expansion in their width.

### Make Corner Blocks

Use corner blocks to give strength to the corners of the doors, and use the router to rout mortises to glue the blocks in place. In order for the corner blocks to fit, they must be five-sided and routed on the outside edges with a ⅛" roundover bit to fit the mortises.

### Assemble the Doors

Assemble the rails with the corner blocks in place, using tape on the outside corners and tape pulled tight

The L-shaped door panels fit into the upper and lower door rails before the stiles are glued in place.

Assemble the top and bottom panel sections with #20 biscuits. Spread glue in the biscuit slots and on the mitered surfaces.

from tenon to tenon on the opposite side to pull the joint tight for gluing. Because you are gluing end grain, spread glue on both surfaces. Use the same technique to glue the panel parts together. To assemble the door units, first put the rails in place and then, with glue spread in the mortises, slide the stiles in place. Use bar clamps to pull the stiles tight to the rails while gluing.

## Make the Top

Make the top and base using biscuit joints and #20 biscuits. Make a dado cut into the inside edges of the parts to hold the panel top and bottom in place. Before gluing the top, cut a chamfer on the panel and matching chamfer on the inside edges of the frame where they will be visible on the top; use a sanding block to sand these edges before assembly. When the top and bottom are assembled, use the plunge router to cut mortises for the vertical stretchers to fit. Use the fence on the plunge router to rout the mortises that are parallel with the edge of the top and bottom frames, but use a clamped-in-place guide strip to rout the mortises at 90° to the edge. Cut tenons on the ends to the vertical stretchers to fit the mortises. Plan these parts to be about ³⁄₃₂" longer than the doors to allow for clearance. Cut a ⅛" dado on the inside edges of the back vertical stretchers for the back panel to fit. Using the plunge router, fence and a ⅛" straight-cut router bit, cut the dados in the top and bottom pieces for the back panel to fit. Determine the setting for the fence by using a back vertical stretcher in

With the plunge router and fence, cut the mortises for the vertical stretchers.

Use a jig with nails to locate the holes in the top section for the hinge pins for the fabric wings. Turn the piece over to locate the pin holes for the bottom panel. Then drill the holes using the drill press.

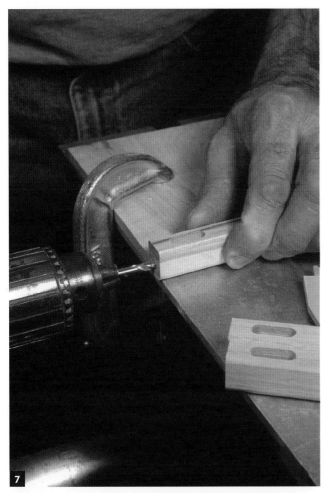

place and measuring the distance to the ⅛" dado. Use a piece of plywood, with the pattern laid out on it for the center points of the brass pins on the pivoting wings, to mark the top and bottom pieces. Use a small drill bit to drill through the marked points, and then, with the template held firmly in place and with the corners glued up, mark the locations for the pins with nails. By turning the template over, you can mark the opposite part with the expectation that the marks will correspond despite any inaccuracies in their layout. Use the drill press and ³⁄₁₆" brad-point bit to drill the holes.

## Make the Base
To make the base and drawer unit, use biscuit-joined corners and size the parts to equal the top and bottom, except for the portion cut away for the drawer to fit.

## Make the Drawer
Before gluing the parts together, cut the ¼" dado for the drawer guide to fit, and cut a chamfer on the inside bottom edges of the parts. Use package-sealing tape to pull the parts together tight, and check them for being square and flat, twisting them a bit or adjusting them before the glue sets. Make the drawer face and base parts from a continuous piece of ash so that the grain pattern and coloration will be continuous around the base unit. Make the drawer using the mortise-and-tenon technique used on other projects in this book. Use a ¼" straight-cut router bit to cut the drawer guide channels in the sides.

## Make the Hanger Support Frame
In making the hanger support frame, mortise the vertical parts for the arms to fit, and then drill into the ends with a ³⁄₁₆" brad-point bit for the pins to fit. I use the Shop Smith as a horizontal borer for this operation, and use a stop-block to control the location of the hole, with the fence clamped firmly in place at both ends to hold the workpiece.

## Install the Raised Inlay
To prepare for the raised inlay, use the ⅛" slotting cutter in the router table, with only about ⅛" depth of cut. Center the height of the cut on the area remaining after the chamfered edges have been routed on the top and bottom pieces. To make the raised inlay, start with

**7**

Use the Shop Smith as a horizontal borer to drill the pin holes in the vertical posts for the fabric wing assemblies. Note the mortises for attaching the arms.

**8**

Use a ⅛" slotting cutter in the router table to rout for the raised inlay to fit.

stock wide enough to cut the tongue while still leaving a control surface, so that the piece will accurately follow the fence and surface of the router table. Use a ¼" straight-cut router bit to cut in on both sides of the strip, leaving the ⅛" tongue at the center. Use a dial caliper to check the thickness of the tongue, making sure it will fit into the slot around the base and top sections.

Use the 45° chamfering bit to rout the profile on the raised strip. If the router bit has an unusually large space between the bearing and cutting surface, as some do, reverse these steps and rout the profile with the strip standing on edge. Use the table saw to cut the bearing surface of the strip away, and cut the depth of the tongue to fit into the slots. Use the cutoff box on the table saw to miter the raised inlay pieces and cut them to length.

Using a low plywood fence tacked in place allows you to safely hold the small stock. Spread glue in the slots, press the pieces in place and use tape to hold them while the glue sets.

Form the raised inlay by routing both sides of the strip with a ⅛" straight cutter, leaving a control surface on both sides of the cut. The center section remaining should be ⅛" thick to fit exactly in the routed channel.

Form the profile of the raised inlay with a chamfering bit in the router table.

Set up the table saw to cut away the inlay strip to finished size, and then miter the strips to length with the cutoff box on the table saw.

# CHAPTER TWELVE

# INLAID WALNUT RING BOX

Woodworking techniques evolve over time. My first boxes were made with simple butt joints and glue. Many have withstood years of use, showing that woodworking can be done to a level of enjoyment and satisfaction with projects less complicated than this box. Like most craftsmen, however, I can't help making things better where I can. The simple mortise-and-tenon technique makes this box strong enough to withstand generations of use, and its bottom panel is free-floating to expand and contract with seasonal changes.

## MATERIALS LIST

| | | |
|---|---|---|
| Ends | 2 | 5/16" x 2" x 2⁹/₁₆" |
| Front | 1 | 5/16" x 1⁵/₁₆" x 2⁵/₈" |
| Back | 1 | 5/16" x 1⁵/₁₆" x 2⁵/₈" |
| Bottom | 1 | 5/16" x 2¹/₁₆" x 2¹⁹/₃₂" |
| Top | 1 | ⅞" x 2⁹/₁₆" x 3" |
| | | *(Resawn at angle from stock; cut to fit dimension of finished box.)* |

**Hardware**

| | | |
|---|---|---|
| Mini barrel hinges | I pr. | 5mm |

## Make the Inlay

Inlay is a good starting point for play and experimentation. This herringbone inlay is simple for a beginner and is often used as inlay banding on furniture. On this box, I decided that two strips would best fill the space available on top.

Glue strips of wood into a larger block. The final pattern will be more interesting if the strips are of varying widths. I frequently utilize offcut strips from other projects. The strips need to have two dimensions roughly in common: thickness and length. Joint the

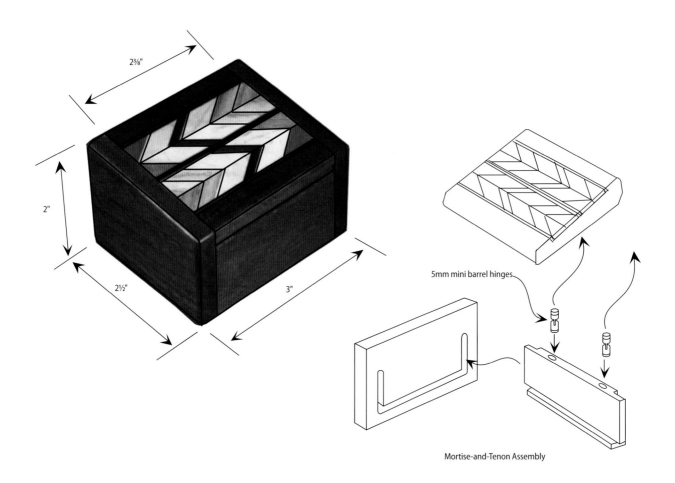

5mm mini barrel hinges

Mortise-and-Tenon Assembly

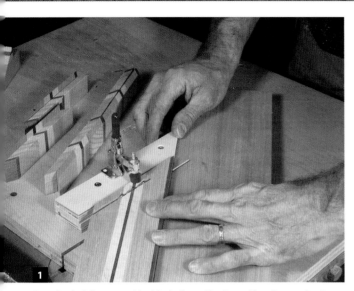

1

To make the inlay, start with a block of wood laminated from layers of various hardwoods. Use a cutoff sled on the table saw with temporary fences nailed or screwed in place.

2

Align the angled pieces that were cut from the laminated block into place along the walnut backing strips. Apply glue to both sides as the parts are laid in position.

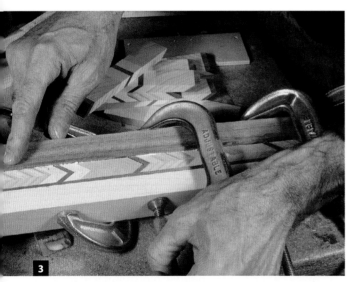

3

Use hardwood backing strips and C-clamps to glue the inlay block together. The backing blocks will keep the assembly straight, saving work later.

4

Before beginning to rip the ³⁄₃₂" inlay strips, I used the jointer to flatten one side of the block. A push stick keeps the fingers safe from the saw blade.

edges of the strips to get good gluing surfaces. Spread glue layer by layer; then, using hardwood strips to distribute the pressure, clamp the strips tightly together. I use a thick hardwood strip on one side to make sure the block will come out straight.

On the jointer, level one side of the block, and square one edge. On the table saw, cut the opposite side of the block so that it is uniform in width. Use the cutoff sled to cut the block into angled pieces. The cutoff sled allows the use of clamps to hold very small parts. Then, using the table saw and rip fence, cut side banding strips about ³⁄₃₂" thick. I used walnut to make the strip blend with the box top.

Arrange the angled pieces on the banding strips, and glue them in place. I apply a layer of glue to the angled piece and

On the router table, use a 1/8" straight-cut bit to rout the mortises for the front and back of the box. The three pieces in the photo show the three-step progression, left to right, for routing the mortises.

To rout the tenons for the box front and back, use a 1" straight-cut bit in the router table. Here I have the safety blocking removed to show the cutter.

Check the fit of the mortise and tenon. A perfect fit will hold against gravity even without glue. Note the safety blocking securely clamped to the router table.

banding strip as they are laid in place. Use the bar clamps and hardwood strips from earlier to clamp the inlay together.

After the glue has dried, use the jointer to clean up one edge of the new inlay block. Use a thin-kerf carbide blade in the table saw to cut strips of finished inlay from the block. The strips should be ripped to about 3/32" thick, allowing for the inlay to have a thickness of at least 1/16" after final sanding.

## Prepare the Box Stock

Cut the rough walnut stock to about 1/4" more than the finished width. Rip the front and back separately from the ends and bottom. Use the band saw and fence to resaw the 1"-thick (4/4) walnut stock. I use a wide blade on the band saw, adjusting the angle of the fence to allow for the natural inclination of the blade.

Plane the walnut stock to 5/16" thick, then joint one edge. Rip the stock to approximately 1/32" and then joint the other side to bring it to the final dimension.

Cut the parts to length on the table saw, using the 90° angle sled or sliding table. Clamp a stop-block to the fence so the parts will be exactly equal in length. Cut the ends to length first, then change the location of the stop-block to cut the front and back. For the bottom panel, loosen the clamp holding the stop-block in place and bump the stop-block over about 1/32". This way the bottom will have just a tiny bit of end-to-end clearance when assembled.

## Cut the Mortises and Tenons

Cut the mortises and tenons on the router table. Because the router bit used for cutting the mortises is a fixed width, cut the mortises first, then cut the tenons to fit.

Install the 1/8" straight-cut router bit. Set the fence 11/32" from the outside tip of the router bit. This measurement is the approximate width of the walnut stock plus 1/32" cleanup allowance, which will be sanded away when the box is completed. Adjust the height of cut to just barely more than 1/8". Cut a test piece, and check the dimensions and depth with a dial caliper. Once you are satisfied the measurements are correct, clamp stop-blocks to the fence to control the width of the mortise. Rout the ends so that the front, back and bottom panels fit. This requires changing the locations of the stop-blocks and routing in three separate operations. Fortunately, the depth of cut and fence position remain the same, and only the stop positions require adjustment.

To rout the tenons to size, use a 1" straight-cut bit, climb-feeding the piece from right to left along the fence. In climb-feeding, the workpiece is moved from right to left between the fence and the cutter. This gives a cleaner cut with little tear-out, but can be dangerous with a dull cutter. Safety blocking is required to keep fingers from being pulled into the cutter. Always rout a test piece to make certain you've set the height of the cutter at ⅛". Test the fit to the mortise by actual fit rather than measuring. Insert the tenon into the mortise. If it goes in easily without forcing but doesn't fall out without shaking it, the fit is perfect and will last many years with just a spot of glue.

Using the same setup as used for the tenons, rout the edges of the bottom panel. Check the fit of the panel to the dados cut into the end pieces, and adjust the fence if necessary.

Use a ⅛"-kerf blade on your table saw to cut the dados in the front and back pieces for the bottom panel to fit into. Set the fence so that the cut will be ⅛" deep and leave a 1" interior space. The front and back will be flush with the bottom when assembled.

In order for the tenons to fit the mortises, small nubs must be cut off. I use the sled on the table saw with the blade lowered so that it just cuts through the thickness of the nub. The stop-block is set so that the saw cut is flush with the routed tenon shoulder.

## Make the Lid

Plane walnut stock to ⅞" thick and 1/16" wider than the planned width of the box. Tilt the band saw table, and adjust the fence to resaw the angled lid. With the help of a straightedge, draw the desired lid shape on the end of the stock. Then compare the pencil mark to where the blade will hit the stock when held up to the band saw.

Make a trial cut, barely penetrating one end of the stock. Turn the stock over to see if the cut aligns. If not, you may have to adjust the fence. When you are satisfied that the cut is at the center of the stock, cut the lid stock into two parts. One part will become the

**8** Using the same setup, shape the bottom panel to fit.

**9** While cutting the dados, a push stick keeps my fingers away from the blade. I also use a block of wood to keep the workpiece against the fence.

**10** Use the sled on the table saw to cut the tenons to width. This involves cutting off the little nub below the dado that the bottom will fit into. Use a stop-block to accurately position the cut.

To cut the channel for the inlay, use a 1" straight-cut bit in the router table. Gradually widen the cut until you reach the desired width. Cut the channel first, then size the inlay to fit.

Adjust the distance between the router bit and fence on the router table, then trim the inlay to fit the channel. Use safety blocking, which was removed for this photo to illustrate the procedure.

Spread glue in the routed channel and press the inlay strips in place.

In my production work, I clamp two lids face to face with a filler strip between them to distribute clamping pressure and to keep the lids from sticking to each other.

lid, but you will need the other part when you drill for the hinges later in this chapter.

## Inlay the Lid

Cut the channel for the inlay to fit into. Use the 1" straight-cut bit in the router table. Raise the height of the cut to just less than the thickness of the inlay. Adjust the fence so that the first cut occurs at the center of the lid. Widen the channel with a second cut. For the final cut, make the channel about ¼" narrower than the combined width of two inlay strips. This last cut is achieved by passing the lid material from left to right on the router table. This keeps the router bit

from grabbing the stock and dangerously pulling it into the cutter.

Cut the inlay strips about ¼" longer than the planned length of the lids, and pass them across the jointer to straighten one edge. Use the jointer to remove enough stock so that the final fitting will leave the border equal on both sides.

Raise the height of the bit in the router table until it is just taller than the thickness of the inlay. Move the fence so that it will cut the inlay strip to size. Safety blocking is a very good idea to keep fingers well away from contact with the router bit. Clamp the safety blocking onto the router table with C-clamps. I prefer

**15**
Trial-assemble your box, then cut the lid to size. A stop-block clamped to the sled fence, adjusting to get the perfect fit, gives accurate results.

**16**
Stop-blocks clamped on the fence of your drill press allow accurate drilling for 5mm mini barrel hinges. Drill precisely in the center thickness of the back piece.

to make the first cut a bit wide, narrowing the width between the cutter and fence on a trial and error basis until I get it right. Spread glue in the routed channel and place the inlay. Clamp the inlay to the lid using a filler strip to distribute the clamping pressure.

## Fit and Hinge the Lid

For this box, I chose the readily available 5 mm miniature barrel hinges which require a 45° chamfer to provide clearance for opening.

Use the sled on the table saw to cut the box top to length. Gauge the dimensions of the box opening with a tape measure, and set the stop-block accordingly. Make the first cut on the right side of the lid, and the second after moving the lid against the stop-block. Trial-assemble the box to test the fit. Bump the stop-block over in small increments to make any adjustments.

With a 5mm brad-point bit in the drill press, adjust the fence so that the bit will drill right into the center thickness of the $\frac{5}{16}$" back piece. Use the dial caliper to check the open length of he mini barrel hinges. The depth of the holes should be slightly less than half the open length of the barrel hinge. Adjust the stop to the right depth, and drill a test piece. Check the depth of the hole with the pin end of the dial caliper. To position the back piece for drilling, clamp a stop-block to the fence. Using a piece of scrap wood, also drill an index piece that will be used to locate the proper position for the stop-block for drilling the opposite hole in the lid. Drill the holes on the left, then the right, using the index piece to adjust the location of the stop-block.

**17**
To set up for drilling the matching holes in the lid, drill an index piece. Check the dimensions with a dial caliper. To help position the stop-blocks, the index piece should start the same length as the back piece. Then cut ⅛" off each end to match the length of the lids.

**TIP:** I usually check wood carefully for cracks and splits that might cause problems in the finished piece. Sometimes, however, they will appear later, or the special character in the wood demands that a particular piece be used despite its flaws. Cracks and splits can be easy to fix. A business card with glue spread on both sides can be slipped into a crack, enabling glue to be spread in hard-to-reach places. Often a small chisel will be needed to widen the crack for the card to be inserted. When the card is pulled out, it will leave glue on both surfaces so the split can be clamped closed until the glue has set, and with modern adhesives, glued joints are often as strong as the wood itself.

**18** I've stacked two lids face to face, eliminating the need to change the drill press table angle to conform with the sloping lid. I suggest using the scrap saved from shaping the lid earlier to form a square block to drill into.

**19** Use a squeeze bottle to apply glue to the insides of the mortises, and assemble the box.

In order for the lid hinge holes to align with the holes in the back piece, allow for the lengths of the tenons and the lid clearance. Move the fence on the drill press slightly more than ⅛", or use a ⅛" shim with a piece of paper or business card stock to provide for clearance. Forming a block, bring together the lid and the scrap saved from shaping the lid. Adjust the depth of the hole. You can drill deliberately less than depth and then lower the depth by increments. Drill another index piece so that the opposite hole can then be drilled without the shims and card stock.

To provide clearance for opening, rout a 45° chamfer on the back sides of the back and lid. Use a ¹⁄₁₆" roundover bit to soften the top edge of the box front. If you wish to sand the inside of the box, do it now before the box is assembled.

## Assemble the Box

Use a glue syringe for the mortises and areas where the box front and back will contact the ends. Fit the front and back pieces to the bottom, and insert the tenons and panel ends into one box end first, then the other.

Insert the hinges into the box lid. The hinges are sometimes tight enough that no glue is required; however, if your hinges go in without much pressure, place a dab of glue in the hole. Position the lid, and insert the hinges in the back of the box, opening and closing the lid to check the clearance and that the box is square. Adjust the box by squeezing corner to corner if necessary.

## Finish the Box

Set up the band saw at the same angle used for resawing the lid, but adjust the fence to allow for the width of the box. Pass the box between the fence and blade, trimming the excess material from the ends. For rough sanding, use the 6" x 48" belt sander with a coarse belt. Sand the ends flush with the top. Moving to finer grits, sand the top, front, back and bottom of the box.

Open the box and, with the inside of the box lid against the fence, rout the inside edge of the lid with the ¹⁄₁₆" roundover bit. After changing to a ⅛" roundover bit, rout all the edges of the box except for the front edge, which will be gently rounded as the box is orbital-sanded. Use the orbital sander to finish-sand the box, gently rolling the corners and edges. I start with #180-grit, then go to #240 and finally use #320-grit. Finish the box with Danish oil.

**20**

After the glue has set, tilt the band saw table to the same angle used for resawing the lids to trim away excess wood from the box ends. The ends should be nearly flush with the lid.

**21**

Use the stationary belt sander to sand the box ends flush with the ends, bottom and lid. Start with #100-grit and work down to #150 before moving to the orbital sander.

**22**

On the router table, shape the inside edge of the lid with a ¹⁄₁₆" roundover bit.

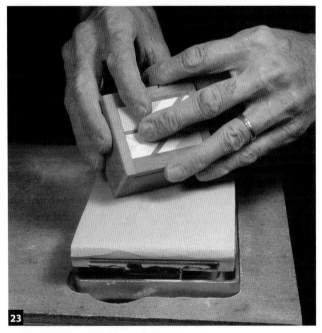

**23**

After using a ⅓" roundover bit on all edges of the box, use the orbital sander to sand the surfaces smooth.

# TRIANGLE RING BOX

Ienjoy figuring out new and simple ways to make things. It doesn't matter to me whether someone has done it before as long as I can have the pleasure of discovering it for myself. This ring box is made using a template and a simple jig to hold parts in place as a series of routing operations is performed. This same technique could be applied to a variety of shapes and sizes. Once the fixtures are made through a few simple steps, the box can easily be replicated in a variety of woods.

# MATERIALS LIST

| Base | 1 | 1" x 3⅜" each side Cut from 3"-wide stock |
|---|---|---|
| Top | 1 | ½" x 3⅜" each side Cut from 3"-wide stock |
| Inlay | 1 | ⅜" x 2" x 2" Or larger |

| **Router Platform and Template** | | |
|---|---|---|
| Platform | 1 | ¾" x 8" x 11" Plywood |
| Feet | 2 | ¾" x 5" x 8" Plywood |
| Template | 1 | ¼" x 8" x 11" Masonite or plywood |
| Dowels | 4 | ¾" x 1¼" Hardwood |

## Make the Routing Jig

This box uses a routing jig, a template-following router bit and an inlay routing set consisting of a ⅛" router bit and guide bushings. The templates are aligned with dowels that fit into holes drilled into the jig. This way the template can be removed for subsequent placement of parts. With imagination and a variety of layered templates, this technique can be expanded to make more complicated designs.

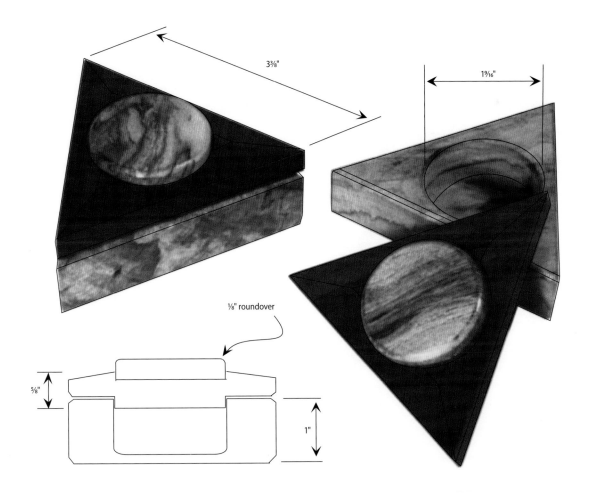

3⅜"

1⁹⁄₁₆"

⅛" roundover

⅝"

1"

Clamp the routing platform to the workbench. The holes provide for accurate alignment of the layered templates.

Screw through the template stock into hardwood dowels, so the template will be easy to remove and replace over the workpiece.

Tack a temporary fence to the table saw sled when cutting the body of the ring box.

Use the sled to cut the box bodies and lids to equal size.

## Make the Routing Platform

To allow you to clamp the platform to the bench without interfering with the jig, attach feet to the underside of the platform. Drill ¾" holes in the corners of the platform for the dowels.

The template stock should be tempered hardboard or Masonite. Cut the template to the same dimensions as the routing platform. Drill holes in the corners for screws in the same position as the ¾" holes in the routing platform. Place ¾" dowels in the platform holes. Place the template piece on top, aligned with the corners. Attach the template to the dowels with wood screws. Countersink the screws so they won't interfere with the movement of the router.

## MAKE THE TRIANGLE RING BOX

By simply changing router bits, you can use a single template for the interior shape, the lip of the lid, the space for the inlay and the inlay itself.

### Make the Box Base

To cut the triangle shapes with the table saw, use a sliding table or sled and a temporary tack-in-place fence to set the angle of cut.

In the center of the template board, drill a hole about ¼" larger in diameter than the size desired for the interior of the box.

Trace the hole onto the router platform so that it lines up with the hole in the template, then pencil the

Drill a large hole in the center of the template stock to use as a guide for shaping the interior space and the lid, as well as making and fitting the inlay.

Trace the circle from the template onto the routing platform, and then lay out the position of the box body in pencil.

Position stop-blocks around the box body to hold it in place. Attach the stop-blocks to the routing platform with brads or screws.

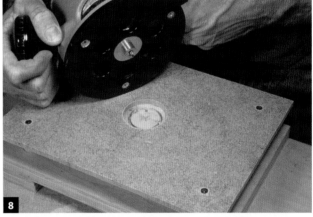

Use the router inlay set to begin routing the inside shape of the box. This should be done with the brass bushing in place. Rout only about ⅛" deep, forming a lip that will be followed to form the inside of the box.

position of the triangle around the circle. Place the triangle piece over the circle, and attach blocking to hold the triangle in place.

Over the triangle piece, set the template onto the platform. With a ⅛" bit cutter and an inlay guide bushing with brass bushing mounted on it, rout the circle into the top of the triangle piece. Rout to a depth of at least ⅛".

This will outline the shape of the box interior, providing a guide surface for the next step.

Insert a bowl-cutting bit or dado bit into your plunge router. Remove the waste inside the box base to form the interior space. A standard router can be used but will require frequent depth changes. The cut must

be made deep enough for the bearing to contact the edge defined in the earlier operation before routing the outside portion of the interior space.

## Make the Lid

Remove the box base from the guide blocks, and put the lid in its place, bottom facing up. Before routing, apply a layer of tape to the inside edge of the template. This will keep the lid from fitting too tightly. Remove the brass bushing from the guide bushing set and with the ⅛" router bit, rout the perimeter of the template. Be careful to hold the guide bushing against the edge of the template.

**9** Use the bowl-cutting bit with the guide bearing in the plunge router to continue forming the inside of the box. Lower the cutter into the center of the box and move toward the sides until the bearing contacts the edge formed by the inlay router set. Make the cut in several steps, taking time between steps to remove waste.

**10** To rout the lip on the lid, remove the brass bushing. With the lid held in the router platform, lower the router into the template. Hold the guide bushing firmly to one side.

**11** To remove the additional waste around the lip, remove the template. Arrange pieces of the same thickness as the lid to support the router. Cut toward the lip as you control the router freehand.

**12** If needed, use a small chisel to clean up the cut.

Remove the template; this routing operation will be performed freehand. To provide router support, arrange wood pieces of the same thickness as the lid around the guide blocks. With a straight-cut bit adjusted to match the depth of cut on the lip, rout away the waste stock at the three corners. Use a small chisel to clean up the cut.

## Inlay the Lid

Turn the lid over, exposing the top, and replace the template. With the guide bushing and brass bushing in place, rout the recess for the inlay piece to fit into. Rout to a ⅛"

depth, moving in circles to remove all the waste stock within the space defined by the template.

Place some inlay stock in the template assembly. It will help if the inlay stock is cut to fit tightly within the holding blocks on the routing platform. Place double-stick carpet tape on the bottom of the inlay piece to keep it from moving. Remove the brass bushing from the guide bushing, and lower the depth of cut on the router bit so it equals the thickness of the inlay stock. Hold the guide bushing against the side of the template, gently lowering the router bit into the stock. Following the template, free the inlay piece from the surrounding material.

**13** Remove the brass bushing; rout the inlay piece to fit. Hold the router tightly to the perimeter of the hole in the template. Use double-stick carpet tape to hold the center piece in place.

**14** Use the table saw to shape the lid, adding interest to the finished box. Sand away the saw marks with a sanding block.

## Shape the Lid and Base

With the table saw blade at a 10° angle, cut the top to shape.

Rout the edges of the base and the underside of the lid with a chamfering bit on the router table. This requires changing the height of cut above the router table for the various parts. I prefer a larger cut at the bottom of the box and very small chamfered edges where the lid meets the base. Rout the top of the inlay piece with a roundover bit prior to gluing it in the box top.

Sand all parts prior to assembly. With the lid in place on the box base, start the sanding operation on the belt and disc sander; then use the orbital sander for the finer grits. The chamfers will be best sanded with a sanding block to avoid rounding.

## WORKING WITH "REAL" WOOD

A note of caution: When one gets to the scale of box where a small lid opens and closes to tight tolerances, a woodworker enters the realm where 1/64" or less can make a difference in the look or feel of a thing. We must put aside the tools of measurement and test the fit of the actual parts as the project grows and evolves toward completion. The dimensions offered in these chapters are starting points. It could be a mistake to begin making one of these boxes by cutting all the parts to size.

Using "real" wood adds to the complications. Solid hardwoods continue to breathe, responding to ambient humidity changes in the environment. Dimensions change. What was flat may cup and curl.

It's a darn hard thing to reconcile with a person's woodworking aspirations.

I have a personal inclination toward working with "difficult" woods that come with a history attached. They may have grown up in a neighbor's yard or come "air-dried" from lumberyards where storage conditions were less than ideal. Many of these woods would not be available from normal hardwood dealers, but I like working with these woods. They bring a quality of adventure to my work. They often challenge my self-esteem when things don't work out quite as I expect. It helps to have a go-with-the-flow attitude, to remember not to take myself too seriously. Woodworking is about having fun, right?

# CHAPTER FOURTEEN

# LATHE-TURNED RING BOX

My lathe-turned ring boxes are a way that I make use of the mixed hardwood scraps from my custom furniture making. The material costs me nothing but the inconvenience of having too much clutter in my shop. I seldom stick too closely to plans in my turning, preferring to enjoy the creative play as refined shapes emerge from blocks of wood. You may find, as I did, that making just one design is not enough.

## MATERIALS LIST

| | | |
|---|---|---|
| Base | 1 | Cut from 2½" x 9" stock |
| Lid | 1 | Cut from 2½" x 9" stock |
| Pull | 1 | Turned from ⅝"-square stock |
| Inlay | 1 | ⅛" x 2" x 2" |

With the lathe-turned ring box, the design possibilities are limitless.

# A NOTE ABOUT TOOLS

I use my 1948 model 10 ER Shopsmith lathe and a SuperNova chuck with pin chuck jaws. The SuperNova chuck is designed to lock tightly into a dovetailed recess cut into the workpiece. The recess gives a completed foot to the work without leaving any obvious point of attachment. It also facilitates accurate realignment if the piece needs to go back on the lathe to adjust the fit of the lid. A simple template and dovetail bit are needed to rout the recess in the bottom. Any bit of scrap with one flat side and that is large enough for the dovetailed recess is fair game for turning.

## Making the Box

Select a piece of 2½" x 9" stock from your scrap pile. I prefer fine-textured woods like maple, walnut or persimmon, but sometimes coarser woods like oak or chinkapin can provide interesting contrast. The pieces for the top and bottom need not be the same size, thickness or species of wood. If the stock does not have a flat side and is not large enough to safely pass across the jointer, use the 6" x 48" belt sander to sand a flat spot. For turning the pull, smaller square stock can be used. For the inlay, band saw a ⅛"-thick slice from a scrap of wood of contrasting color.

To make the template, use ⅛" or ¼" plywood or hardboard Masonite. I make my template large enough to allow clamps to hold it in place without interfering with the router. As an option, a smaller template can be held in place with screws. On the drill press, drill a 1¼" hole in the hardboard. The hole need not be precisely 1¼".

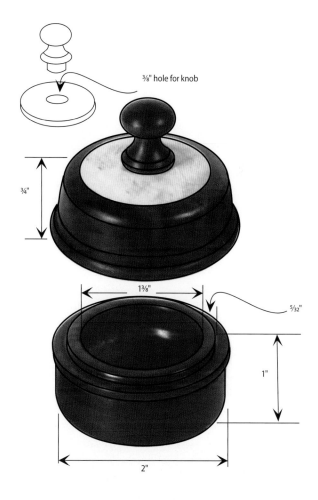

⅜" hole for knob

¾"

1⅜"

5/32"

1"

2"

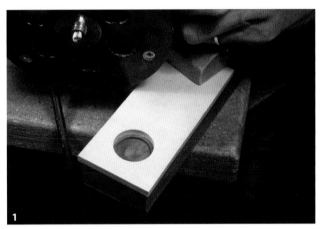

Drill a 1¼" hole in scrap plywood to form the template for routing dovetail recesses. The template will be clamped to the hardwood stock.

On the lathe, shape the inside of the base. Use a skew chisel to form the lip that will hold the lid in place.

Turn over the base and reattach it to the lathe chuck. The slight dovetail recess you left on the inside of the base will allow the chuck to hold it tightly. Use the gouge to shape the bottom of the box.

Sand the base while it is on the lathe. Progress from #150-grit through #320-grit.

Clamp the template in place, and rout the dovetailed recesses in the base and lid. Use a ⁷⁄₁₆" guide bushing and a ⁵⁄₁₆" dovetail bit to rout the recess to a depth of approximately ⅛". Rout the back of another scrap piece for use as a mini faceplate for shaping the inlay. This piece should be surfaced uniformly on both sides. It can be solid stock, ¾" particleboard or plywood.

## Shape the Body of the Box

To make the stock easier to shape on the lathe, cut off the corners with your band saw. Mount the bottom stock in the chuck. Using a small gouge, hollow out the inside of the box. Make a dovetail recess in the first ⅜" to ½" of the opening so that when the box is reversed in the chuck, the dovetailed jaws will grip securely. The opening must be carefully planned not to cut through into the recess on the bottom. Using a skew, cut the shape of the box lip to fit the planned overlap of the lid. Use various lathe tools to shape the upper area of the box bottom. Sand the interior, lip and top surfaces of the base with a succession of sanding grits.

Remove the base from the chuck, and turn it over so the chuck will be able to tighten inside the opening of the box. Check to make sure that the box is on evenly and securely. Use the gouge to shape the lower portion of the box bottom, then sand.

## Make the Inlay

I use a piece of sugar maple with a dovetail recess cut into the back to hold it to the lathe as a mini faceplate. Attach

Use calipers to gauge the box lid as it is formed; first the inside shape, and then after the box is turned over in the chuck, the space for the inlay to fit.

Use inside calipers to check that the interior space in the lid matches that of the base.

the ⅛"-thick veneer inlay to the mini faceplate with double-stick carpet tape. Mount the mini faceplate in the chuck, and cut the inlay piece to size with the skew.

To shape the inside of the lid, repeat the sequence used for the base. Once again, the opening must widen, forming a dovetail shape, in order for the chuck to fit. Use calipers to make sure the size of the opening conforms to that of the bottom. Use the skew to cut the lip wider so the base will fit the lid.

Remove the lid from the chuck and remount it with the chuck gripping the inside. Use the gouge to form the shape of the lid. Then use the skew to form and adjust the recess for the inlay to fit into. Carefully glue the inlay in place. With the inlay in place, use the skew to level the inlay with the surrounding wood. Sand the lid and, using the skew chisel, cut the hole in the top for the pull to fit into.

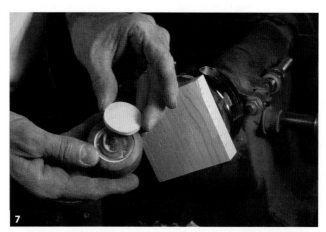

Spread glue on the inside of the recess cut in the top surface of the lid and press the inlay piece in place. After the inlay is glued in place, the lid can be put back on the lathe for final shaping and to cut the hole for the pull to fit.

## Make the Pull
Cut ½"-square stock to a 4" length. Mount the stock, using the SuperNova chuck as a pin chuck, and turn it to a pleasing shape. To cut the shape, use a small gouge and the skew chisel. Use the parting tool to form the tenon for the pull to fit in the lid. Check the size with calipers.

On the lathe, sand the pull through a range of grits. Start at #100-grit, and finish at #320. Finally, leaving enough of the tenon to fit the lid, use the skew chisel to cut the pull from the remaining stock.

Glue the pull in place, and use a wiping varnish or Danish oil to bring the colors of the woods to life.

Shape the pull. Use your imagination to create something that contributes to the overall design of the box.

# CHAPTER FIFTEEN

# HALF-TURNED BOX

This box, with its soft curves, is perfect for presenting a string of pearls or for storing small treasures. Each box is half of a complete turned form, made more interesting by the way it presents a profile of the turned shape. I made my boxes from cherry, walnut and sassafras, turning the boxes on the lathe, two lids at a time. The interior shape of the base is created using a bowl-cutting router bit with a bearing mounted on the shaft, following a template cut out on the scrollsaw.

## MATERIALS LIST

| Bases | 2 | 1" x 4½" x 9" |
|-------|---|---------------|
| Lids | 2 | 1" x 4½" x 9" |

**Hardware**

10mm Barrel Hinges (2 pr)

## Making the Faceplate Assembly and Template

Cut two pieces of ¾" plywood to size: one exactly square, the other exactly half the width of the larger one. The square piece will become the wood faceplate. The smaller rectangular piece will become the template for routing the base and drilling the hinge holes.

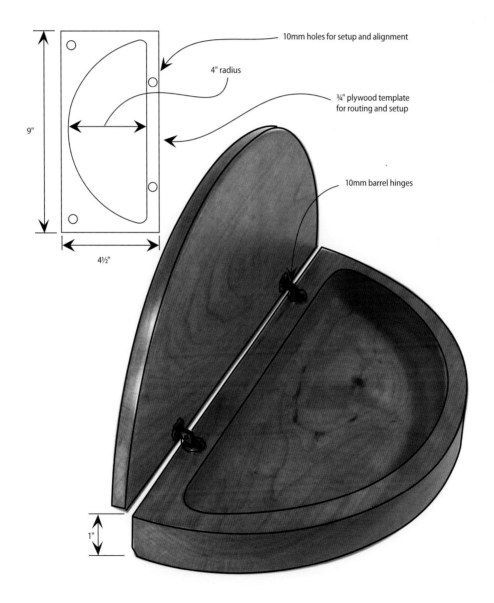

10mm holes for setup and alignment

4" radius

¾" plywood template for routing and setup

10mm barrel hinges

9"

4½"

1"

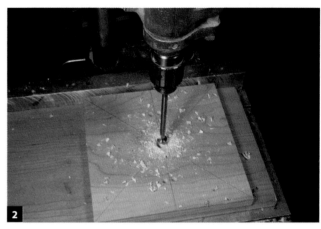

Drill a hole the same size as the lathe arbor at the center of the wooden faceplate to achieve accurate alignment to the cast-iron faceplate.

Assemble the wood faceplate to the cast-iron faceplate by putting them on the lathe arbor in reverse order.

Use stops clamped on the drill press fence to position the holes for indexing the workpieces to the faceplate assembly. The 10mm drill is sized to fit the 10mm barrel hinges that will attach the lid to the base of the box. Use the same setup to drill the matching holes for the template.

Find the center point of the wood faceplate, marking from corner to corner with a pencil. This point will be used when drilling to align the wood to the cast-iron faceplate of your lathe. Using the dimensions in the template diagram, mark the holes for the dowels that will fit the hinge holes, and hold the lids to the faceplate assembly. For this technique to be safe and efficient, the wood has to be sound, without splits or cracks that could allow the wood to separate from the faceplate assembly. If you're uncertain about the soundness, an additional screw can be used through the faceplate, firmly anchoring the wood. This is also a good option if

you're unsure of your ability to turn the wood without digging in too abruptly with the lathe chisels.

On the drill press, drill 10mm holes into the wooden faceplate and template. Use a stop-block to align the holes in both pieces. Drill an index piece to help in setting up to drill the opposite holes. Open the hinge, and measure the distance between the barrels to determine the clearance required.

To attach the faceplate, first drill a hole the same size as the lathe arbor at the center point of the faceplate block. Slip the faceplate block over the arbor of the lathe, then the faceplate. Using the arbor to assure their alignment, use

4

Use a straight-cut router bit to begin defining the interior space for the template, moving the template piece between stops along the router table fence. Note the pencil sketch showing the planned interior space. As you move the workpiece back and forth, gradually raise the cutter until it penetrates through the top. Another option is to turn the piece over, end for end, between raising the router bit, and stopping when the cuts join.

screws to attach the faceplate block to the faceplate. If your lathe has a Morse taper faceplate attachment, you must align the parts by careful measuring. Then, the faceplate assembly can be removed, reversed, and firmly attached to the lathe with lightly sanded ⅜" dowels that fit into the 10mm holes. Taper the ends of the dowels slightly so the lids can be removed after turning.

## Rout the Template

Use the router table and a straight-cut bit to form the back inside edge of the template. Use stops to control the movement along the fence, and raise the router bit in increments until it penetrates through the template. To reduce the number of steps in raising the cutter, and to leave the router bit safely buried in wood until the final cut, cut in on one side of the template and then the other, finally having the two cuts meet at the center.

## Define the Box Interior

Use a scroll saw to define the interior space of the box. The interior space can echo the exterior shape, or can be freeform to offer a surprise. Use a sanding drum or small grinder in the drill press to clean up the interior shape of the template.

5

Use the scroll saw to further define the interior space.

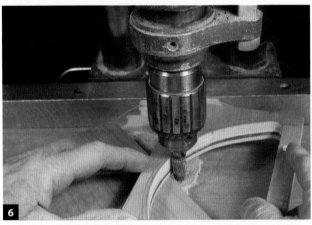

6

Smooth the interior space in the template using a rotary or handheld rasp, a small sanding drum or coarse sandpaper.

7

Use the 10mm hinge holes to set up the stops and fence on the drill press for the hinge/indexing holes in the lid and base parts. You may set up to drill one end and then move the stop to drill the other, or set up two stops to control drilling the matching holes.

**8**

Drill the 10mm holes into the lid and base parts, changing the location of the stop for drilling the opposite hole. Check the depth of the hole with your dial caliper, making certain the depth is equal to half the total length of the barrel hinge.

**9**

Use double-stick carpet tape and ⅜" dowels to attach the lids to the face plate. The ⅜" dowels will need to be sanded smaller to fit in the 10mm holes. Before turning the lids on the lathe, use the band saw to cut away most of the waste, providing a nearly round turning blank.

## Turn the Lids

First, cut the lid and base parts to dimension. Each part should be the same finished size as the template. Then use the template to set up stops on the drill press and to set the position of the fence. Set the drill to penetrate half the length of the closed barrel hinge. If the tops and bottoms are the same thickness, they can be drilled with the same setup. Use a dial caliper to check the depth. Then, drill the hinge holes for the tops and bottoms of the boxes.

Squeeze the box tops into place on the faceplate assembly and, after trimming to shape on the band saw, mount it on the lathe. As you work, remember the locations of the hinge holes, and avoid cutting too deep in those areas. No exact shape is required, so this is a good time to play until you find an interesting one.

Sand the lid smooth, starting with #100-grit, then #180, #240 and finally #320-grit. Then pry the finished lids from the faceplate assembly.

## Make the Base

Insert short dowels into the holes on the template to hold it securely to the box bottom. Use a plunge router and a template-following bowl bit to hollow out the space. Gradually lower the cutter in small increments, taking time between operations to remove accumulated router dust. When you reach the bottom of the planned cut, move the router in small circles to flatten the bottom.

Remove the template and, using ⅜" dowels, press the lid and base together. Use the band saw to cut the outline of the box bottom to rough shape, and with either a sander disc in your table saw or a belt/disc sander, sand the edges even.

Finally, soften the edge where the boxes open and close with a ¹⁄₁₆" roundover bit in the router table. Sand the inside of the lid and the top of the base with the orbital sander. Install the hinges before sanding the back and front edges of the box. Finish the box with three coats of Danish oil.

**10** Use a variety of lathe tools to shape the lids. Remember the locations and depth of the hinge holes to avoid cutting through the lids.

**11** To connect the template to the box base stock, use ⅜" dowels sanded to fit the 10mm holes. With a bowl-cutting bit and guide bearing mounted on the router bit shaft, use a plunge router to gradually cut away the interior of the box. After roughing out most of the interior, rout in very small circular patterns to smooth the bottom to make it uniform.

**12** Alignment pins placed in the hinge holes attach the lid and base for final shaping. You can band saw the bottom shape to conform to the lid or use your imagination.

**13** If you wish to make the lid conform to the base, a sanding disc in the table saw will sand them flush. A very light touch is required to avoid damaging your hard work.

# CHAPTER SIXTEEN

# BRACELET BOX

One of my favorite boxes I've made is the tea box. The tea box had a crotch-figured walnut top, locked or finger-jointed corners and a narrow inlay band of cherry and maple. This box is another offering that uses that beautiful combination. The crotch figure is formed where major limbs intersect, giving an intense multidirectional grain pattern that is dense and highly reflective. Crotch-figured walnut is very heavy, difficult to work and among the most beautiful of woods. It is also very common. I often have pieces of crotch-figured walnut left over from furniture making where its tendency to be less stable is a disadvantage and its striking figure is hard to use. Crotch-figured walnut is most commonly available in low-grade lumber, making it a special reward for the bargain hunter willing to dig through the woodpile.

## MATERIALS LIST

| | | |
|---|---|---|
| Ends | 2 | ⅜" x 1½ " x 2⁵⁄₁₆" |
| Front | 1 | ⅜" x 1½" x 9 |
| Back | 2 | ⅜" x 1½" x 9 |
| Top | I | ⅜" x 1½" x 8⁷⁄₁₆" |
| Bottom | 1 | ⅛" x 1½" x 8⁷⁄₁₆"<br>*Baltic birch plywood* |

### *Hardware*

¾" Brusso solid brass hinges with built-in stop (1 pr.)

## PREPARE THE STOCK

Resaw the walnut into thin panels for the top and sides on the band saw. Use the most highly figured walnut for the top panel. Crotch walnut is prone to warping, so flatten one side on the jointer before ripping. After ripping, plane it down with the planer. A thickness sander is helpful in bringing crotch walnut to final thickness because crotch walnut has a tendency to tear out in planing. The side panels can be book matched to bring continuous grain around the box.

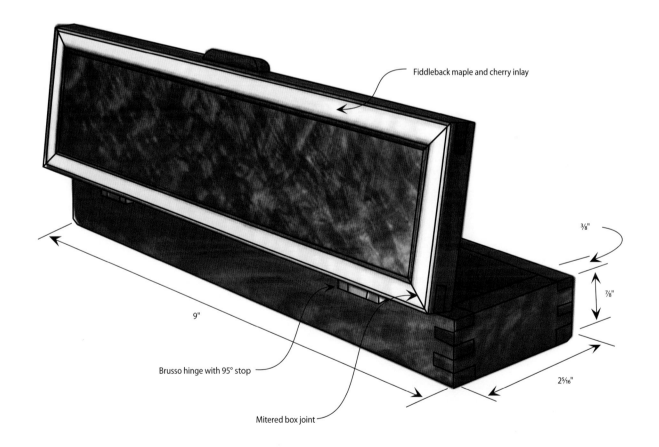

Fiddleback maple and cherry inlay

⅜"

⅞"

9"

2⁵⁄₁₆"

Brusso hinge with 95° stop

Mitered box joint

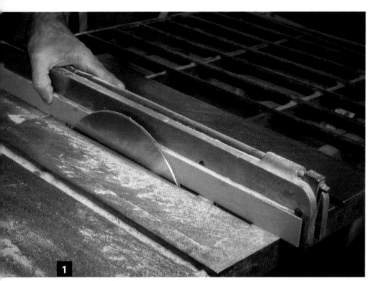

1

Use the tapered sanding disc in the table saw to thickness the inlay strip.

## Make the Inlay

Making inlay bands requires a great deal of accuracy in milling the thickness of parts. I have found that thin parts can more easily be sanded to dimension than planed. This is because when stock gets very thin, it may lift into the planer knives, giving an uneven thickness. Sanding exerts a more even pressure against the stock, allowing more accurate dimensions to be achieved. I often use a disc sander to thickness stock, particularly when it is very thin or highly figured and prone to tear out during planing. A disc sander for the table saw is a good alternative.

Rip thin strips of maple and cherry. Use the disc sander to sand the parts to thickness, and then glue them together. I use thick hardwood backing blocks to make certain that the glued-up strip is flat.

# MAKING A BOX-JOINT JIG

This box-joint jig looks complicated but is fairly easy to make. The sliding work cable and base are cut from a single piece of ¾" plywood. The dados for the hardwood runners to fit are cut before the plywood is cut into the two sections of the jig. There are no exact dimensions required for making an effective jig. After cutting the two sections from the plywood, an additional dado is required to attach the fence to the sliding table. The runners need to be carefully planed to fit: tight enough to give good control, but loose enough to slide easily. Use screws to attach the router base to the bottom of the jig, countersinking the screws to be flush with the top of the jig base, and wood screws to attach the sliding runners to the jig base.

After attaching the router to the base, use a straight-cut router bit to cut though the base to provide clearance for the bit and collet. This is done with the upper section out of the way, and by gradually raising the router in a series of cuts. Next, put the upper section in place. With the ¾16" router bit installed in the router, gradually raise the bit while sliding the upper section of the jig over the cutter. This will open up the clearance for the router bit to pass. You may find it necessary to rout additional clearance with a larger router bit for the ¾16" bit to raise high enough

through the sliding table. Use hardwood to make the fence for the jig. I used a ¾16" brass pin to form the stop that controls the position of the workpiece. Drill a hole for the pin before installing the fence on the sliding table. Its location should be ¾16" from the router's line of cut. Use wood screws to attach the fence to the sliding table.

To fine-tune the jig for a perfect fit, remove the screws holding the fence to the sliding table and bump it over very slightly to compensate for fingers being too tight or too loose.

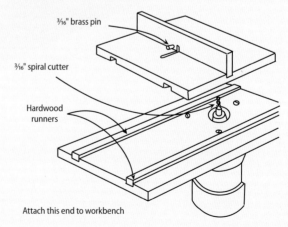

¾16" brass pin

¾16" spiral cutter

Hardwood runners

Attach this end to workbench

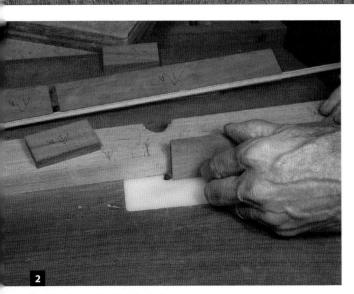

**2** Rout the channel for the inlay to fit.

**3** Spread glue in the routed channel.

**4** Press the inlay into the routed channel.

**5** Clamp the parts edge to edge while the glue dries.

Sand both sides of the inlay block on the disc sander, adjusting the fence to bring the block to the desired thickness. Use the dial caliper to check that the dimensions are the same on both sides. If not, adjust the angle of the disc. Try to remove equal amounts from both sides of the block so that the maple will have equal cherry borders. Then, using the thin-kerf blade in the table saw, rip 3⁄32"-thick inlay strips from the block.

## Inlay the Sides

Cut the box parts to length. With a ¼" straight-cut router bit in the router table, rout the channels for inlay strips to fit into. Be sure to adjust the fence to place the channels at the centers of the box parts. If the fit is not perfect on the first try, widen the space between the cutter and fence very slightly and rout the parts again.

Cut the inlay strips to the required lengths. Spread glue in the channels, and press the inlays in place.

Proceed with the balance of the cuts on the ends, front and back.

Arrange the box sides in pairs, and clamp them edge to edge to make sure pressure is evenly distributed to the inlay.

## Finger Joint the Corners

To cut the finger joints, I use a shop-made router jig and a spiral cutter. The spiral cutter reduces tear-out and gives more accurate cuts.

Push a piece of scrap stock against the alignment pin, and make a through cut. Then, with the scrap piece reversed, clamp it in place on the box joint jig fence.

With the scrap guide piece in place, make the first cuts in the end pieces. The bottom edges must be pushed up tightly to the guide piece. After the first cuts

Make your first cut on a piece of scrap, then turn it over and clamp it to the box-joint jig. This will position the box ends for the first cuts.

Note the completed front piece with stock remaining for the mitered corner.

Use the miter sled to trim the miters on the ends and the front and back pieces. A stop-block controls the position of the cut.

are made, remove the guide piece and make the remaining cuts, lifting the stock over the guide pin for each successive cut. Cut the fingers in the front and back parts of the box, stopping short of the final cut to allow for the mitered corners at the top of the box.

## Miter the Corners

I believe mitered joints on finger-jointed boxes give a more finished look, and they allow the use of inlay banding.

Use the table saw and sled to cut the miters on the box ends. The mitered cut on the inside of the box must align with the depth of the finger slots. This tends to be a trial-and-error process. A stop-block clamped to the fence allows the cut to be changed in very small increments. Set the height of cut at just barely the amount required to cut through the fingers on the box ends. The same setting can be used for mitering the front and back pieces.

Reverse the angle of the fence, and cut the opposite sides. Once again, this is a trial-and-error operation. Check the fit of the box ends to the front or back to see that the miter closes tightly. Use a straight chisel to clean up the cuts.

## Make the Top and Bottom Panels

Set up stops on the router table fence to control the length of cut. Using a 1/8" straight-cut bit, rout the dados for the top and bottom panels to fit the sides. To keep the dado invisible from outside the box, use the fence stops to restrict the length of the dado.

Use a 1" straight-cut bit in the router table to form the tongues on the top panel to fit the dados in all four sides. For the heavily figured walnut, I make relief cuts with the table saw to ease the router's work and to make it easier to control the workpiece. Check the fit of the top panel in the dados.

Cut the bottom panel to size and check its fit in the dados. If its too tight, use the same setup on the router table to cut the edges of the panel to fit.

## Assemble the Box

Sand the inside of the box. Then use a glue syringe to apply glue to the surfaces of the fingers. Put the top panel and bottom in place, and assemble the box parts.

Carefully observe to make sure the miters pull tightly together. The space around the top panel should

To cut the miters on the front and back parts, make sure the blade height equals the thickness of the remaining fingers on the box ends. Make a series of cuts sliding the workpiece in toward the stop. Note the finished miter joint.

Rout for the top and bottom to fit. The stops on the fence prevent the dado from appearing on the outside of the box.

Use a squeeze bottle to apply the glue carefully to the fingers as you assemble the box around the top and bottom.

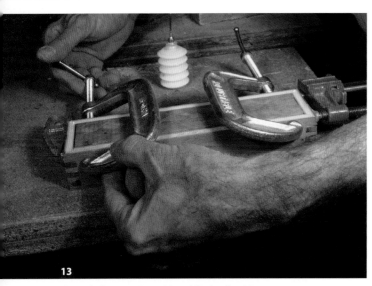

**13**

Clamp the box parts in position while the glue dries.

**14**

Use the tapered sanding disc in the table saw to shape the top of the box. The arbor is tilted to face the top of the box. I shape my boxes by moving the fence toward the disc in three steps.

**15**

To cut the lid loose from the base, set the band saw fence so that the blade will cut at the joint between fingers.

be even all around. Clamp the box tightly together while the glue dries.

## Finish the Box

Use the belt and disc sander to sand the fingers flush with the box sides. Use the disc sander in the table saw to taper the top panel and top edges. On my box, I did this with a 10° angle setting on the saw, moving the

fence a little at a time until I achieved the angled top surface I wanted.

Cut the lid from the bottom on the band saw. Align the cut so that the box separates right on the line between fingers. Before making the cut, check and adjust the band saw fence to allow for variations in the tracking of the band saw blade that could ruin all your hard work. Sand away the band saw marks with the belt and disc sander. Be careful to sand both side to side and front to back equally.

Use the ⅛" straight-cut bit in the router table to create the mortise for the lid tab to fit. Sliding the box lid between stops controls the position and length of cut. Use a ¾" straight-cut bit to rout the mortises for the hinges. Set the height of cut to slightly less than half the closed thickness of the hinge. Use the fence to determine the location of the hinges on the box lid and base.

Holding the box lid and base together, sand all the outside surfaces of the box. Sand the edges very slightly with a sanding block. Apply the Danish oil finish, carefully rubbing between coats. When the oil has dried, install the hinges.

With a ⅛" straight-cut bit in the router table, form the mortise for the lid tab to fit. Stop-blocks are used to control the length of cut.

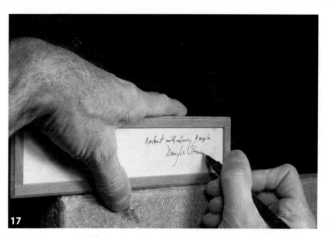

In signing my work, I like to give acknowledgment to the woods used.

The application of an oil finish brings beautiful wood to life. This is one of my favorite parts of the process.

# WEDDING RING MUSIC BOX

The first wedding ring music box that I made was for a man whose future bride had a dream about a small box with a musical movement that played the "Theme From Ice Castles." This dream box was sized and lined to hold their wedding rings. He asked me to make it for her as his special wedding gift. It is a very special honor for a craftsman to be asked to help bring someone's dream to life. I chose elm for this box and inlaid it with walnut, figured maple and pecan. The simple inlay technique uses shop-made oval templates and an inlay guide bushing set that is readily available from most woodworking stores and catalogs.

# MATERIALS LIST

| | | |
|---|---|---|
| Ends | 2 | ⅜" x 2¼" x 3½" |
| Front | 2 | ⅜" x 2¼" x 6 |
| Back | 2 | ⅜" x 2¼" x 6 |
| Interior divider | 1 | ³⁄₁₆" x 1" x 3" |
| Top | 1 | ⅜" x 3" 5½" |
| Bottom | 4 | ⅛" x 3" x 5½" *Baltic birch plywood and template stock* |
| Inlay veneer | 1 | ⅛" x 3" x 5½" *Walnut* |
| Inlay veneer | 1 | ⅛" x 1" x 1½ *Walnut* |
| Inlay veneer | 1 | ⅛" x 3" x 5½" *Curly maple* |
| Inlay veneer | 1 | ⅜"-diameter plug *Cherry* |
| Feet | 4 | ⅝" x ¹¹⁄₁₆" x 4" |
| Slip feathers | | Cut from ⅛" stock |

### Hardware

¾" Brusso brass box hinges with built-in stops (I pr.)

Music Movement (your choice of tune)

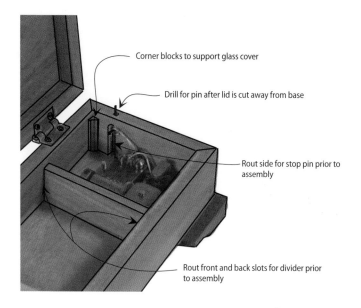

Corner blocks to support glass cover

Drill for pin after lid is cut away from base

Rout side for stop pin prior to assembly

Rout front and back slots for divider prior to assembly

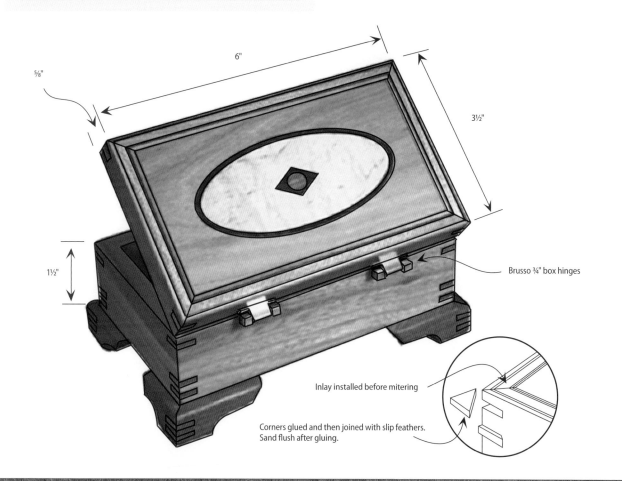

6"

⅝"

3½"

1½"

Brusso ¾" box hinges

Inlay installed before mitering

Corners glued and then joined with slip feathers. Sand flush after gluing.

Use a straight-cut bit in the router table to cut the channel for the inlay.

After gluing, clamp the inlaid parts together in pairs to hold the inlay tightly in position.

Cut the miters for the box parts using the miter sled on the table saw. Clamp a stop-block in place to control the length of parts.

## Make the Box

To make good use of material, resaw 4/4 elm stock, and plane it to a ⅜" thickness for the sides and top panel. Make the inlay banding using the same technique shown in making the bracelet box in chapter sixteen. Rout the sides for the inlay to fit, glue the inlay in place. Cut the miters using the miter sled and stop-block on the table saw.

Rout one end for the music box shutoff spring mechanism. Also rout the inside front and back of the box for the divider that will form the music box compartment.

Dado the ends, front and back for the top and bottom panels to fit. This can be done on the router table with a ⅛" bit or on the table saw with a ⅛"-kerfed blade.

## Make the Inlay Templates

Draw an oval shape on paper (I used my computer's drawing program), and then stick the drawn shape onto the template stock with adhesive.

On the scrollsaw, cut the oval shape into the original template. The scrollsaw will leave some rough edges to even out and smooth with sandpaper. To finish the template, use a dowel with coarse sandpaper.

Clamp or screw this original template to another piece of plywood stock of the same dimensions. With a ⅛" bit, and using the inlay guide bushing with the brass bushing in place, rout a smaller version of the original template. This secondary template will be used to rout the space inside the walnut border to fit the figured

Rout the box end for the shutoff rod for the music movement. Next, using the same technique, rout the front and back for the interior divider to fit.

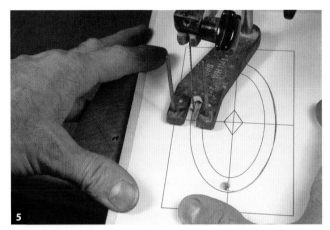

**5** Glue an oval shape to scrap plywood stock. Use a scrollsaw to cut the oval shape into the primary template. The larger oval allows for the guide bushings, which will reduce the size of the final inlay piece.

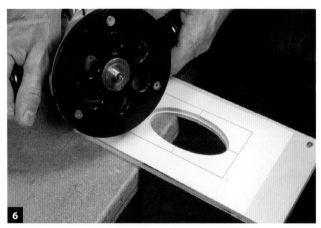

**6** Use the primary template to form the secondary template. I used screws to attach them to each other for routing.

**7** Changing templates and guide bushings allows the various inlay parts to fit within each other. Use the brass bushing over the guide bushing to rout the inside shapes, then use the guide bushing without the brass bushing to cut the part to fit. Use scrap stock brad nailed to the backs of the templates to hold the workpieces in position for routing.

**8** Hold the guide bushing firmly to the side of the template as the bit is lowered into the stock. Hold the router firmly to the edge of the template as you follow around the oval shape.

maple within. To accurately position the stock for routing, nail strips to the back side of the templates. The space defined by the strips should be sized exactly to match the panel for the top.

Make a diamond template using the same techniques as used for making the oval templates. Cut the diamond shape with the scrollsaw, then clean up the edges and finish the corners with a straight chisel.

In order to keep the inlay material from moving around while routing, the veneers must be taped to backing panels with double-stick carpet tape. The backing panels need to be cut to the same dimensions as the top panel to keep them from moving. Cut an extra panel at this time to serve as the box bottom.

## Make and Install the Inlay
On the band saw, rip the inlay stock from solid wood. Before cutting, pass one side across the jointer to provide a good gluing surface. Leave the other side rough, to be finished when the box is sanded.

9

10

Use a third template for routing the diamond shape that appears at the inside of the oval. Double-stick carpet tape holds the veneers in place as the small pieces are cut from the surrounding stock.

Use a ⅜" bit in the drill press to form the space for the center circle to fit. Use a ⅜" plug cutter to form the round inlay piece.

Insert the top panel into the space defined by the strips on the back of the original template. With the brass bushing in place, rout the stock away, forming the recess for the inlay to fit into. The depth of the cut should be just a bit less than the thickness of the veneers cut on the band saw.

Cut a piece of maple veneer slightly longer and wider than needed, and use carpet tape to attach the veneer to a backing piece. Insert the veneer with the backing piece into the smaller template. Rout the shape of the maple inlay using the guide bushing without the brass bushing in place.

Using the same template, insert a backing piece with walnut veneer taped in place. Then, using the guide bushing with the brass bushing in place, rout the inside shape into the walnut for the maple to fit.

Remove the walnut center piece, and replace it with the maple one. The walnut banding is very fragile; it

## MAKING A SLIP-FEATHER JIG

I use a simple jig on the router table to cut the slots in the corners of boxes for slip feathers to fit. To make this jig, I first make a new low fence to fit the router table. It attaches at one end with a wing nut and at the other with a C-clamp. Using hardwood blocks, build a saddle form to fit around the fence, leaving room on one side to allow for the thickness of the ¼" plywood used to form the base of the jig. There are no exact measurements required for making a working jig, but it may be helpful to size it to allow for the largest size boxes you will plan to make.

Using the table saw, cut a hard wood block to form the cradle that holds the box for slip feathering. For making square boxes, the block should be cut using the saw arbor tilted to 45°. Use small screws or brads and glue to assemble the parts of the jig as shown in the drawing. I used screws on mine so that it could be taken apart and

modified as necessary. In using the jig, cut short sections of hardwood dowels to position the box for cutting the slip feathers. This keeps you from having to change the position of the fence for various cuts.

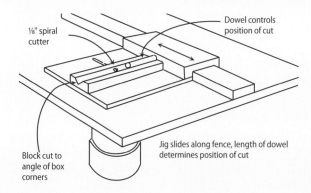

⅛" spiral cutter

Dowel controls position of cut

Block cut to angle of box corners

Jig slides along fence, length of dowel determines position of cut

will help give strength if the maple piece is glued in place before the next cut.

Change to the larger template, and insert the walnut-and-maple piece with backing into the space formed by the strips on the underside. Remove the brass bushing, and rout the walnut piece to fit into the top of the panel. Now, with the top panel in place and the brass bushing on the guide bushing, rout the channel around the edges of the top panel for the inlay pieces to fit. It may require a very light sanding on some edges for the inlay to fit the recess. Glue the inlay in place, with backing pieces to prevent marring the back of the panel with the clamps.

Rout the diamond shape inside the oval using the diamond template. After removing the brass bushing, use the same template with a backing piece to rout the veneer to fit the diamond. Fitting the veneer inside the diamond will require some handwork, either rounding the points of the diamond or using a chisel to finish the cut in the oval.

With a ⅜" bit, drill for the cherry plug to fit inside the diamond. After the plug is glued in place, the top panel can be sanded on the belt and disc sander.

## Shape the Feet

To make the feet for the music box, stock must be milled to shape prior to assembly. This requires a 1.1" straight-cut bit on the router table. Use stops to control the movement of the parts. To define the shape of the feet, gradually move the fence in small increments. Making a relief cut on the band saw can speed up the operation, reducing the number of router setups. You will find that if you make all the cuts from the right to the left, moving along the fence and reversing the stock at the middle of the cut, dangerous tear-out at the end of the cut can be avoided.

## Prepare for Assembly

Prior to assembly, make the interior divider. Square the routed slots in the box front and back square with a small chisel. Sand the interior surfaces of the box sides, top panel, divider and bottom.

## Assemble the Box

Put glue on the mitered surfaces, and assemble the box around the top and bottom panels and the interior divider. The section that will be cut apart to form the feet can also be glued up now. Clamp the pieces together. On a small box like this, you can use rubber bands or band clamps.

Use the ¾" straight-cut bit in the router table to form the shape of the box feet. I cut away most of the waste with the band saw before routing.

Assemble the box parts around the top, bottom and divider. Spread glue on the mitered surfaces, assemble, and then clamp the box securely.

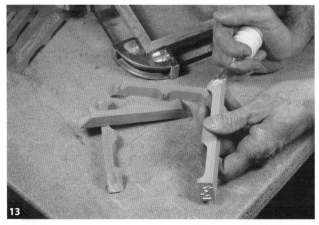

Spread glue on the miters, and clamp the box feet parts together until the glue dries.

Use the slip-feather guide on the router table to cut for the corner wedges to fit. Use stop pieces of varying lengths to control the positions of the slip feathers.

Use the same technique to slip-feather the corners of the feet.

Spread glue into the slots, then press the slip feathers in place.

Use the band saw to cut the top of the box from the bottom. This cut must be planned carefully to allow for the interior divider and the music stop pin.

After cutting the assembled units apart and using a roundover bit in the router table to give them shape, hand sand the feet. Here I'm using the orbital sander with the power turned off as a sanding pad.

Sand the inside contours of the feet with a dowel wrapped in sandpaper.

**20**

Use ⅛" dowels to attach the feet. Glue the feet in place first, then after the glue has dried, use the drill press to drill for the dowels to fit. After trimming the dowels flush with the surrounding material, use a sandpaper-wrapped dowel to finish the job.

**21**

Shape the lid tabs on the router table. The center part is routed to fit the ⅛" mortise cut into the box lid. Use a ⅛" roundover bit to shape the tabs before they are cut to length.

**22**

Hold a set of tabs together for routing the ends. It's OK to make more than you need.

**23**

After the box is sanded and oil finished, rout for the hinges to fit. Clamp stop-blocks to the router table to control the length of the cut, then change the location of the stop-blocks to rout the opposite sides.

Using the slip-feather jig on the router table, cut recesses for splines to fit in the corners of the box and the feet.

Cut walnut splines, and glue them in place in both the box and the feet. After the glue has set, use the belt and disc sander to bring the splines flush with the surrounding surface. After the splines have been sanded flush, use the band saw to cut the top of the box away from the base. Use the belt and disc sander to smooth the band saw cuts.

Rout a ⅛" mortise in the front of the lid for the lift tab.

## Finish and Attach the Feet

Use the table saw to cut the individual feet apart from the assembled group. Set the miter slide at a 45° angle and the saw arbor at 90°. This operation can also be performed using the table saw fence with the saw arbor tilted, but there is some risk of kickback.

Shape the edges of the feet with the ⅛" roundover bit in the router table. Then sand them with a dowel wrapped in sandpaper. Spread a bit of glue where the feet will contact the box, and carefully position the feet in place. After the glue has dried, drill for ⅛" dowels to

Use a Vix bit in the electric drill to drill for the screws to fit the hinges.

Make a paper template for installing the music movement; I use business card stock. Mark the locations of the holes with an awl.

I use a small brad as the bit when drilling for the stop pin on the drill press. When drilling the holes to attach the movement, use a wood block under the box to prevent splitting out the underside of the plywood bottom.

connect the feet to the body of the box. After trimming the dowels flush with the surrounding material, use a sandpaper-wrapped dowel to finish the job.

As a final step in the attachment of the feet, use a fine rasp and then a sanding block to gently shape the areas between the feet.

## Make the Pull

To form the outside profile, shape a strip of walnut using a ⅛" roundover bit. Use a ⁵⁄₁₆" straight-cut router bit to form the tenon.

Cut the walnut strip into short pieces. Then, holding them together on edge, use the ⅛" roundover bit in the router table to shape the ends of the pulls. Holding the walnut pulls together as a block allows them to follow the fence and keeps them from tipping as they are routed. I always make extra pulls to use for other projects.

Use the sled on the table saw to finish forming the shoulders on the tenons. Then cut them apart, being sure that the tenon length matches the depth of the mortise cut in the box lid.

## Install the Hinges

Sand and finish the box with Danish oil. To mortise for the hinges to fit, use a ¼" straight-cut bit in the router table. Use the fence and stop-blocks to position the box parts over the cutter for routing the hinge mortises. You will need to adjust the position of the stop-blocks for cutting the opposite sides.

Rout a test piece to check the accuracy of the setup. Square the corners of the hinge mortises with a straight chisel. Drill for the hinge screws with a Vix bit.

## Install the Music Box Movement

Mark the locations of the holes for the music box movement with an awl onto a paper template.

Drill the required holes, using a block of wood underneath to keep the plywood bottom from splintering around the holes. Use the screws provided with the movement to attach it to the box. On the drill press, position the fence and stop-blocks to drill for the music box stop pin. It may take some trial and error to bend the wire for the music box shut-off mechanism.

# CUTTING MITERS

Cutting accurate miters can be a challenge. Getting the angle just right is often a trial-and-error process and can be frustrating. I use two different sleds, or sliding tables, on the table saw to assist in cutting miters. The first is designed to use the table saw with the angle at 90°. This is used for narrow stock or stock that must be cut standing vertical on the table saw (**Figure 1**). To make this sled, I use a carpenter's square to set up the angled parts. This ensures that each side will be perfect in relation to the other. Even if one side were off ½° or more, the other would compensate, giving a tight-fitting miter.

To make this sled, first mill hardwood runners to the size of the miter guide slots on the top of the table saw. Check their fit. They should slide freely but have no side-to-side play. Use screws to attach one runner to a piece of ¾" plywood, making sure the runner is square to the front edge of the plywood. Place the other runner in the miter guide slot on the table saw. Using screws, attach the plywood to it. Use a 45° tri-square to help position the first 45° strip to the sled. Use screws to hold it in place.

Raise the blade of the table saw. Sliding the sled on the tabletop, cut into the sled, cutting the angled strip to length. Use a carpenter's square to position the matching angle fence on the opposite side, and attach it to the plywood with screws.

The second sled (**Figure 2**) uses the saw arbor tilted to 45°. This sled works best for wide stock. To make it, begin making the first sled. But when the runners are in place, turn the sled over. Using a ¾" dado set in the table saw, make a cut in the sled top at 90° to the runners. The dado is for the fence to fit into. Plane the fence material down to ¾", and hold it in place with screws from the underside.

You'll find the first sled is easy to use because it requires the table saw blade at the normal 90° setting. Stop-blocks can be clamped in place to accurately cut pieces to length. The second sled requires the saw arbor to be tilted to 45°. I use a tri-square to check the angle, and I always make the first cut on scrap stock. These two sleds will make your mitering on the table saw easy and accurate.

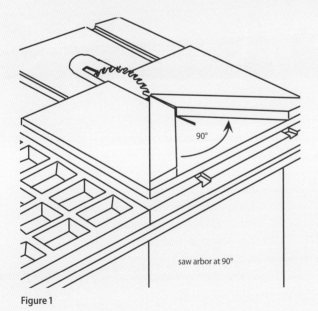

90°

saw arbor at 90°

Figure 1

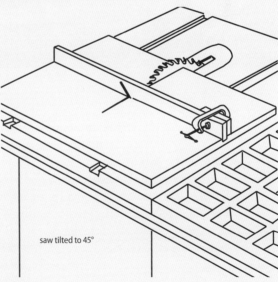

saw tilted to 45°

Figure 2

# CHAPTER EIGHTEEN

# WINTER WOODS BOX

When I was a child in Memphis, Tennessee, I often went on family outings to Shelby Forest, a nature reserve on the Mississippi River. Walking in the woods there in the park is one of my earliest memories and continues to be a source of inspiration in my work. These days, I live in a small clearing in the forest just north of Eureka Springs, Arkansas. Our home sits on a narrow shelf, with a steep mountain to the north and a deep "holler" to the south. Walking in our woods has now become one of my daughter's earliest memories as well. This box is my attempt to share the tactile experience of a walk in the woods in winter.

## MATERIALS LIST

| | | |
|---|---|---|
| Ends | 2 | ⅜" x 2⅞" x 6¹⁄₁₆" |
| Front | 1 | ⅜" x 1¾" x 8⅝"<br>*Includes ³⁄₁₆" tenons* |
| Back | 2 | ⅜" x 1¾" x 8⅝"<br>*Includes ³⁄₁₆" tenons* |
| Lids | 2 | ⁹⁄₁₆" x 3⅛" x 8¼"<br>*Resawn from<br>contrasting ¾" stock* |
| Base sides | 2 | ⅝" x 1⅛" x 10⅛" |
| Base ends | 2 | ⅝" x 1⅛" x 7⅛" |
| Box bottom | 1 | ⅛" x 6⁵⁄₁₆" x 9⁵⁄₁₆"<br>*Baltic birch plywood* |
| Drawer sides | 2 | ⅜" x ⁹⁄₁₆" x 8¾" |
| Drawer back | 1 | ⅜" x ⁹⁄₁₆" x 5¾" |
| Drawer bottom | 1 | ⅛" x 6⁵⁄₁₆" x 9⁵⁄₁₆"<br>*Baltic birch plywood* |
| ***Hardware*** | | |
| Hinge pins | 4 | ³⁄₁₆" dia. x ³⁄₁"<br>*Cut from ³⁄₁₆" brass rod* |
| Lid stops | 4 | ⅛" dowel x ½"<br>*Cut from ⅛" dowel* |
| Pulls | 2 | ⁵⁄₁₆" x 1½" x 3¼"<br>*Cut from stock* |
| Reeds | 18 | *For the pulls* |
| Copper wire | 2 | 4"<br>*12-gauge* |

## Choosing the Wood

I often have small pieces of various hardwoods left over from my custom work. Many are highly figured but available in very limited quantities, enough for a box top but not for sides as well. The richness of black walnut makes the perfect frame for lesser-known American hardwoods. In this box, I used spalted pecan that has been resawn and bookmatched. The reed, an almost fragile material, invites a gentle touch. The winter woods box also has a secret drawer hidden in its base.

## Prepare the Stock

To make the best use of your materials, cut the stock to width before resawing and planing. Using the band saw and fence, resaw the walnut stock into pieces of equal thickness. Plane these to ⅜" thick. Then, joint one edge of the stock, and rip on the table saw to the required dimensions. I usually rip the stock to ¹⁄₃₂" oversize and then bring it to final size by passing it on edge through the planer. Another option is to joint the opposite side, so you won't have saw marks to sand away. Next, resaw the material for making the lids. Plane these to ⁹⁄₁₆" thick, and joint one side.

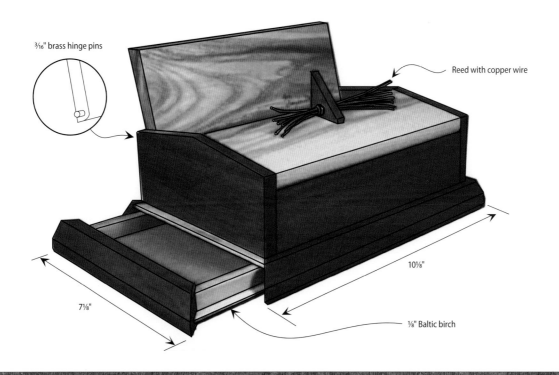

³⁄₁₆" brass hinge pins

Reed with copper wire

10⅛"

7⅛"

⅛" Baltic birch

1

Use a straight-cut bit in the router table to form the tenons on the box fronts and backs. Note the relief cuts made on the table saw to ease the router's job and to prevent it from pulling the work piece into the cut. This is particularly needed when making a large cut or when working with hard wood like this figured walnut.

2

After the tenons are cut to fit the mortises, carefully measure and mark the locations for the hinge pins to fit the box ends.

## Make the Box Body

With the cutoff sled or sliding table on the table saw, cut the box body parts to size. Don't cut the lids to size yet. It is best to wait and get your final dimension from the trial-assembled box body.

To rout the mortises in the box ends, use a ⅛" bit in the router table. Set the height of the cutter ³⁄₁₆" above the height of the table so that the mortises will be ³⁄₁₆" deep. Check the depth with the dial gauge. To allow for glue and variations, I usually cut about ¹⁄₂₈" deeper than required. The fence should be set to allow for some waste to be sanded away after assembly.

Use a 1" straight-cut bit in the router table to cut the tenons on the front and back pieces. Before cutting the tenons, I often make a relief cut on the table saw. This helps keep the wood from being grabbed pulled into the router and scaring the daylights out of me, as it eases the cut. This precaution is required when making a large cut or when working with very hard wood like figured walnut.

Make a test piece before cutting your stock. Test the fit in the actual mortise. If the tenon enters easily, but does not fall out when you hold it up, you have a good fit.

To trim the tenons to width, use the table saw with the sled to cut away corners at the bottom of the fronts and backs. Align the first cut with the tenon shoulder. Then for the second cut, turn the piece on end, and readjust the stop on the fence. This will cut away a small corner, allowing the tenon to fit the width of the mortise.

## Fit the Lids

Assemble the box ends, fronts and backs with the tenons in the mortises. Measure the exact length of the opening. Using the sled on the table saw, cut the lids to fit the opening. I generally cut the lids to exactly the length measured and then make a second cut after bumping the stop over just slightly. This gives clearance for the lid to open and close without scraping the sides.

To mark for the hinge pin holes, use a straightedge along the top front edge of the trial-assembled box to mark the location of the box lid, and then mark in ¼" for the position of the pin. Measure up from the edge of the box front ¼" plus ¹⁄₁₆" for clearance for opening and closing. These measurements will give the center points for the holes on the box ends. I also mark the edges of

**3**

Align the points marked for drilling on the drill press, adjusting the fence and then clamping stop-blocks in place to position the holes accurately.

**4**

With an ⅛" bit in the drill press, set up stop-blocks and drill for the lid stop pins to fit.

**5**

After positioning one stop-block, drill through a piece of scrap wood and use it as an index piece to set up the opposite stop-block so the hinge pins on opposite ends will be in perfect alignment. Note the box end on the lower right has already been drilled while the opposite stop-block location is being determined.

**6**

Using an old carbide blade, cut the hinge pins to length on the table saw. I use 3⁄16" brass welding rod. Gently round the ends of the hinge pins on the belt sander to make assembly easier.

the holes so that it is easier for me to see that I have accurately set up the drill press with the brad-point bit.

Use a drill press to drill the hinge pin holes in the end pieces. I use a 3⁄16" drill bit that I broke off shorter and reground to a brad point in order to eliminate flex. Use stop-blocks and a fence to control the position of the holes. To make sure that the holes on opposite sides are aligned, drill an index piece that will help to reset the stop.

With a ⅛" bit in the drill press, mark and drill for the lid stops. Use the drill press fence and stop-blocks to control the position.

Use 3⁄16" brass welding rod for the hinge pins. With an old carbide blade in the table saw and using a cutoff sled and stop-block, cut the hinge pins to length. Slightly smooth the ends of the pins by rolling them against the 6" x 48" belt sander. This will make the box easier to assemble.

Drill for the hinge pins to fit the lids. To hold the lids vertical for drilling, make a fixture to fit a standard drill press. My ShopSmith works as a horizontal borer, but this fixture is just as easy and accurate to use, and it works on a standard drill press. I always start with a test piece and check the position of the hole carefully with

**7**

Before the box lids are cut to length, mark the matching resawn panels so the face and back sides will not get confused.

**8**

Use a trial-assembled box to check the fit as the lids are cut to length. I use a crosscut sled on the table saw and use a stop-block to make certain the matching lids are the same length and fit to close tolerances.

a dial caliper. Adjust the position of the stop to drill the opposite side.

Now, the lids can be cut to their final width. Slip the ⅛" birch stop pins in place in the box ends. Then, with the hinge pins in place, fit a lid to an end piece. Mark the center line where the two lids will meet, and mark the box lid at that same point. Then with a sliding T-bevel, transfer the angle formed by the lid and box end to the table saw. Use the mark on the lid to help set the fence to cut the lids to the required size. After cutting the opposite lid to the same size, check the fit where the two lids meet. If they are too tight and do not allow a bit of space for expansion of the material, adjust the table saw fence just a bit narrower, and cut the lids again.

## Assemble the Box

Before assembly, rout mortises in the lids for the pulls to fit. Use a ⅛" straight-cut bit in the router table. Adjust the fence so that the cutter will be at the center of the width of the lids. Control the length of cut with stop-blocks.

Use a glue syringe to put glue into the mortises. With the hinge pins installed, fit the front and back tenoned parts into one end. Then carefully align the parts and slip the other end in place. If they fit tightly, no clamping will be necessary. Open and close the lids to make sure that the box is square.

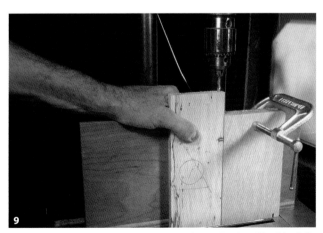

**9**

When drilling for the hinge pins, an accessory clamped to the table of the drill press helps hold the lid while a stop-block positions it.

**10**

After drilling one end of the lid, reposition the stop-block to drill the hinge hole in the opposite end. Note the structure holding the square to the base.

After putting one hinge pin in a lid and fitting it to a box end, use a sliding T-bevel to transfer the angle to the table saw for cutting the correct angle where the lids meet.

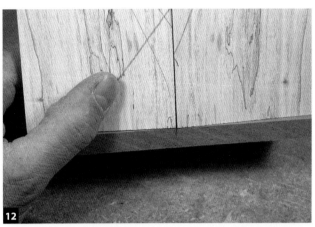

Note the pencil mark at the center of the box end to indicate the width of the cut on the table saw when cutting the lids to width. I use a trial-and-error system to get a good fit, making my first cut wide and then narrowing the distance from the blade to the fence.

Rout for the lid pulls prior to assembly. Stop-blocks clamped to the router table control the length of the cut, while the fence is set to position the mortises equidistant from the ends of the lids.

Assemble the box with glue and clamp as needed.

Use the table saw to trim the box ends to conform to the shape of the lids. Duct tape will hold the lids closed during the cut. Then using the 6" x 48" belt sander, sand the ends level to the lids and sand the ends flush with the front and back.

## Make the Base

Plane walnut stock to size for the base. Then cut the pieces to length using the mitered sled on the table saw. Use a stop-block to control the length of the pieces, changing the location of the stop-block for the two different lengths.

Use a ⅛"-kerfed saw blade to cut the channels for the plywood to fit. These cuts should be ⅛" from each edge.

Cut ⅛" Baltic birch plywood for box and drawer bottoms. These should be sized to fit the space allowed, less about 1/64" each dimension to allow for sliding.

To assemble the base, first sand the birch plywood pieces, gently rounding the edges with sandpaper. Then glue three edges of the top piece and only one edge of the bottom piece to fit in the base dados. Put glue in the dados, and also the corners, before assembling and clamping. Be careful not to

15

Use the table saw, or the band saw tilted at an angle, to cut the box ends to shape. Taping the lids closed with duct tape keeps them from coming in contact with the saw blade. Plan your cut to allow for some stock to be sanded flush on the stationary belt sander.

17

After the base parts are cut to length, use the table saw with a ⅛"-kerf blade to cut the dados for the box bottom and drawer to fit.

16

Use the mitered cutoff sled to cut the base parts to length. Note the C-clamp holding a stop-block in place to control the length of the parts.

glue the piece that will become the drawer front except where it fits to the drawer bottom. Clamp the pieces together.

Trim the base to shape on the table saw with the arbor tilted to 22½°. The base must be upside down when cutting. First cut the sides and then the ends.

Use hardwood stock to form the drawer sides and back. Rout the top edges with a 1⁄16" roundover bit in the router table. Then use the 45° cutoff sled to cut the angles and the straight 90° cutoff sled where the drawer

18

Use glue in the dados as the base is assembled around the box bottom and drawer. Glue the drawer bottom to the drawer front, but not the sides. Glue the box bottom to all the rest of the parts, but not the drawer front. Do not glue the miters intersecting the drawer front. This will allow the two parts to slide apart to open.

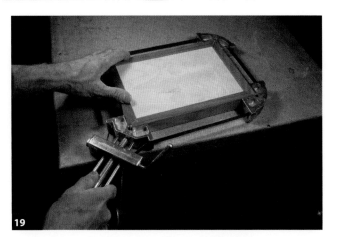

19

Use a band clamp to hold the parts together as the glue sets.

20

Use the table saw, with the arbor tilted to 15°, to cut the base to shape. Be careful to check which side is up before cutting. The base should be upside down on the table saw to be shaped properly.

21

Use the 1" straight-cut bit in the router table to shape the tenons on the ends of the lid pulls. Set the height of cut to just less than the depth of the mortises In the lids. Check the fit of the tenon to the box lid. Rather than using test pieces in this operation, I just plan to make more than are necessary and adjust the fence or router height as needed.

22

Drilling the holes in the lid pulls can be done either before or after shaping the tenons. I use a ¼" brad-point bit in the drill press and position the hole slightly off center.

sides meet the front. I use a jig to hold the parts in position for gluing and nailing in place with brads.

## Make the Pulls

Cut and plane stock to ⁵⁄₁₆" thick, and then cut it to width and length for the pulls. As in making the tenons for the box front and back, use the 1" straight-cut bit in the router table to form tenons on the ends. This can be done either before or after the holes are drilled into which the reeds will fit. Use the cutoff sled on the table

saw to trim the tenons to length. Next, using another cutoff sled, set up an angled fence and stops to cut the pulls to shape.

## Fit the Box to the Base

Use a straight-cut bit in the router table to trim the box to fit the base. Set the height of the bit to ⅛" so that it will fit down into the base. I always make my first cut on a test piece so I can check the fit before routing on the assembled box. Trim each side to fit, then check

**23**

Cut the tenons to the proper width on the table saw. Use the sled and a stop-block clamped to the fence to position the cut.

**24**

The final shaping of the pull is done using an angled sled on the table saw. This sled, with no permanent fence, allows temporary fences to be tacked in place. The angled sled also allows for the use of clamps to hold workpieces securely.

**25**

Use clear glue to attach the box to the base. Then use masking tape to clamp the parts together as the glue dries.

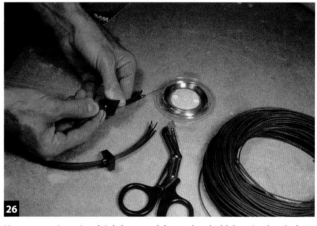

**26**

Use copper wire twisted tightly around the reeds to hold them in place before gluing the pulls into the box lids.

the fit with the base. Adjust the fence as needed to get a good fit.

Use the orbital sander to sand the box parts. Lightly sand the edges with a sanding block to smooth. Hand sand the pulls with sheets of sandpaper.

Apply three coats of Danish oil finish. I apply one heavy coat of oil and wait about half an hour before applying the second. After the second coat starts to get a bit sticky, I rub it out with a dry cloth. Wait about 24 hours before applying the third coat and, like the second coat, rub it out when it just starts to get sticky.

Use clear all-purpose glue to attach the box to its base. I use masking tape to hold the parts together as the glue dries.

Cut eight or nine pieces of reed to fit through the ¼" hole in each pull. Dye the reed with dark brown Rit fabric dye before cutting it to length. Push a 4" piece of 12-gauge copper wire through the hole after the reeds are in place. Carefully wrap the wire tightly around the reeds on both sides of the hole, first one side and then the other, reversing directions of twist on the two sides. Use carpenter's glue applied in the mortise to hold the pull itself in place. Use flocking material or Ultrasuede as a lining for the base drawer and the inside of the box.

# MY ROUTER TABLE

My router tables are quick and easy to make – just a router turned upside down, bolted to a piece of ¾" plywood and clamped to the work bench. When I'm done with it, I can unclamp it and put it away, saving precious floor space in my crowded shop. I use a pivot fence with my router tables, which gives a great deal of accuracy and is so easily made that I can make them in different configurations as I need them (see **Figure 1**). The pivot fence is simply a piece of wood with a hole through it for a bolt. The bolt attaches it to the router table, and the other end is secured by a C-clamp.

## Make the Inserts

To safely accommodate various router bits, make inserts that fit the hole in your router table through which the bit emerges. I usually get around to making the inserts sometime after the table has been in use for a while.

First, cut several square inserts on the table saw to the exact same size. Round the corners to a ¼" radius by standing them together on the router table with a ¼"-radius ball-bearing roundover bit. You can use ¼" maple, plastic, birch plywood or Lucite. Use a fence to cover most of the cutter and to help guide the pieces squarely into the cutter. Never do an operation like this with a router held freehand.

## Make the Template

With eight strips of ¼" plywood, construct a template around the inserts. Overlap the plywood at the corners. This will build a template the exact same size as the inserts (see **Figure 2**). Glue and nail the pieces to each other while surrounding the inserts.

If you want it to look neat, you can cut the plywood pieces to the exact length needed. Remember to make the template large enough so there is room for clamps on it as well as the router base.

## Rout the Table for the Insert

Clamp the template in place on the table, and rout for the inserts to fit. I use a ½"-diameter mortise cleanup bit. Adjust the depth of cut so that the bit protrudes beneath the template equal to the thickness of the inserts. Provided the ¼"-radius cutter is precise, the inserts and recess routed for them should fit perfectly. If they are just a bit tight in the corners, sand them a bit or touch them up with a fine rasp.

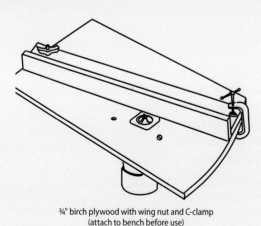

¾" birch plywood with wing nut and C-clamp
(attach to bench before use)

Figure 1

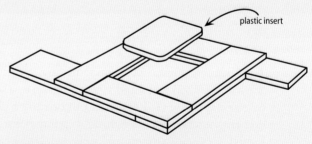

plastic insert

1. Assemble "log cabin" around insert, glue and nail corners.
2. Clamp to tabletop and rout to proper depth with mortise cleanup bit.

Figure 2

# CHAPTER NINETEEN

# MEN'S JEWELRY BOX

In designing a box, I often imagine how it will be used, where it will be placed and where a person will stand when opening it. These considerations impact its usefulness and appearance. I designed this box to be slightly asymmetrical. With the back lid being thicker, it has a natural stopping point to prevent it from opening too far. No special or expensive hardware is needed. It uses the same hinge method and mortise-and-tenon joinery as the winter woods box from chapter eighteen. The front lid needs to open to full width so as not to block access to the interior. The single pull offers a clear sequence in opening.

## MATERIALS LIST

| | | |
|---|---|---|
| Ends | 2 | ⅝" x 4⅛" x 8 |
| Front | 2 | ½" x 3" x 10½"<br>*Includes ¼" tenons* |
| Back | 2 | ½" x 3" x 10½"<br>*Includes ¼" tenons* |
| Lid | 1 | ⅝" x 3¾" x 10" |
| Lid | 1 | ½" x 3¼" x 10" |
| Bottom | 1 | ⅛" x 6¼" x 10¼"<br>*Baltic birch plywood* |
| Tray | 1 | 1¹⁄₁₆" x 3" x 9⁹⁄₁₆" |
| Tray ends | 2 | ³⁄₁₆" x 1⅛" x 3¹⁄₁₆" |
| Tray dividers | 2 | ³⁄₁₆" x ⅞" x 2¼" |
| Tray supports | 2 | ⅛" x ¼" x 6" |
| **Hardware** | | |
| Lid stops | 2 | ⅛" x ¼" x ¾" |
| Hinge pins | 4 | ¾"<br>*Cut from ³⁄₁₆" brass rod* |

## Choosing the Lumber

I chose white oak for this box because I had some in my shop that was just the right thickness for planing down to make the parts. I have made similar boxes in maple and walnut. As with most of the boxes in this book, I suggest that you use the woods you have at hand, allowing your own lumber-hunting adventures to have as much an impact on your box making as my instructions.

## Form the Box Ends

First, mortise the ends of the box. Use the router table and fence with a ³⁄₁₆" straight-cut bit. Position the mortises with stop-blocks, changing the locations of the blocks for mortising the opposite ends. (The inlaid

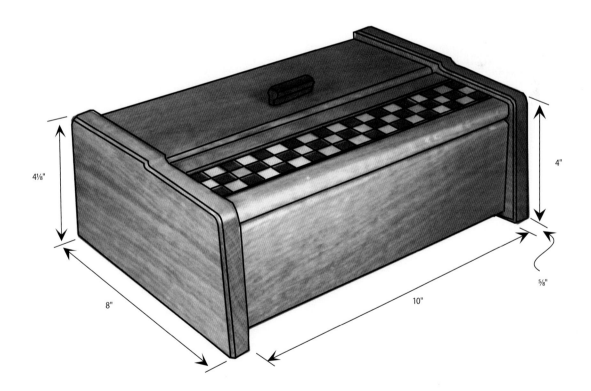

**1** Use the router table to rout the tenons after the mortises are formed in the box ends. Note the relief cut made on the table saw to ease the router's work. This is crucial when making such a large cut. I have removed the safety blocking to give a better view.

**2** Use the router table to form the template that will be used to shape the ends of the box. A stop-block clamped to the surface of the router table controls the length of the cut.

walnut ring box from chapter twelve shows this operation in detail.) To accurately position the opposite mortises, perform the same operation on thinner stock and use that as an index piece for routing the opposite mortise. To avoid breaking the fragile bits, I cut to the full depth of the mortises in two steps. Check the depth of the mortise with the dial caliper.

With a ⅛" straight-cut bit in the router table, rout the positions for the bottom panel, the tray slides and the lid rest. To keep the cuts from extending through the ends of the stock, use the router table for this job rather than the table saw. Please note that the positions of the lid rests are different on opposite ends, allowing clearance for the tray to be removed.

## Make the Front and Back

To form the tenons, first make a relief cut. Use the sled on the table saw to perform this operation. The relief cut will ease the routing process by keeping the workpiece from being pulled into the cut. Use a stop-block to accurately position the cut. Form the tenons themselves on the router table with a 1" straight-cut bit.

Cut the dados in the front and back for the bottom to fit. This can be done either on the router table, with a ⅛" straight-cut bit, or on the table saw, with a ⅛" kerfed blade.

With the table saw and sled, trim the tenons to width to fit the mortises.

## Make the Lids

To make the inlay for the front lid, cut blocks of wood to ½" x ¾" x 1¾". Glue them together in an alternating pattern. Rip to form a ½"x ¾" x 1¾" square stock. Rearrange and reglue with edge banding. Rip thin strips for inlay.

For this box, I chose the easy way out and used an inlay design left over from other projects. If you want ideas for making your own inlay, you might want to start with patterns like that used for the inlaid walnut ring box. These patterns can be a starting point for your own personal experimentation in making inlay.

On the router table, rout the space for the inlay. Set the height of cut just less than the thickness of the inlay.

For this, lay the inlay strip down on the table and check it against the position of the bit. Move the fence to widen the cut so that it nearly fits the inlay strip.

With the table saw sled, cut the angles in the edges of the template.

After all the mortises are cut, use the sled to cut the angles in the box ends.

Use a disc sander to round the top corners of the box end template to shape. I just penciled in the desired radius on the corners and then carefully sanded. A little bit at a time gives the best results.

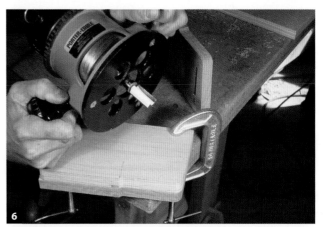

With the template and box end carefully aligned and firmly clamped to the workbench, shape the box ends, using a template-following router bit. I prefer to trace the shape on the workpiece and remove most of the waste with the band saw before routing.

Joint one edge of the inlay strip. To size the inlay to fit the routed channel, adjust the fence position on the router table and raise the height to the straight-cut bit.

Spread glue in the routed channel, and press the inlay in place. Spread the clamping pressure and prevent marking the box lid by using clamping blocks.

Sand the inlay flush with the surrounding wood. This can be done with a belt sander, or on the 6" x 48" stationary belt sander. Check your progress regularly to avoid changing the thickness of the workpiece.

Trial-assemble the box to test the fit. Measure the opening, and cut the box lids to exact length. The sled and stop-blocks on the table saw work well for making sure both lids are exactly equal in length. After cutting the lids to a perfect fit, adjust the stop on the sled a very slight amount to make the final cut, providing side clearance for opening and closing.

To provide clearance for opening, rout the outside edges of the box lids with a ¼" radius roundover bit in the router table.

Rout a small mortise for the pull on the back lid. Use the ⅛" straight-cut bit in the router table. This is similar to routing for the pulls in the winter woods box except that the wood grain is oriented parallel to the fence.

This photo shows all the parts ready for assembly. Note the mortises, the tray-support pieces already glued in place, and the dados for the bottom panel.

Assemble all the parts at one end, then apply glue to the mortises for the opposite end, and clamp the box together.

## Shape the Ends

The ends of the box are shaped to conform to the lids' change in thickness. To do this, and to give the box tops their round profile, make a template exactly the same size as the box ends. Use a scrap of ¾" plywood left over from another project.

Adjust the router table fence to ⅛" and with a straight-cut bit, rout the template between stops. Perform this same operation on the box ends, remembering to turn one end upside clown so that the box ends will form a matched pair.

Set up either a miter gauge on the table saw, or a sled with the desired angle, and cut both the template and box ends to finished shape. Then, on the band saw, cut a small radius on the top corners of the template. I used a radius of about ⅜", but this need not be exact. Finish the band sawn radius smooth with the disc sander.

Using the template, pencil the shapes of the radius on the box ends, and band saw away the excess on the outside of the line. One at a time, clamp the template over the ends, and rout the shapes to conform to the template. Use the template-following router bit.

## Hinge the Lids

This technique is explained fully in chapter eighteen on making the winter woods box. Carefully lay out the position of the hinge pin on the box end, and then, with the drill bit in position to drill the hinge hole, adjust the fence and stop-blocks on the drill press. Remember to drill the same hinge holes in the template so that you will have a record of the setup for future boxes. You will need to change the setup of the stop-blocks for drilling opposite ends.

Drill the hinge-pin holes in the lids, again using the same setup as shown for the Winter Woods Box. The stop-block will have to be adjusted for drilling the holes for the opposite ends of each lid. Then cut a ³⁄₁₆" brass welding rod to length for the hinge pins. Measure the holes in both the box end and lid with a dial caliper. Add them up to get the length of the pins required.

## Assemble the Box

Rout all the edges of the box ends, front, back and lids with a 45° chamfering bit. Then sand all the parts, progressing from coarse to extra fine. Start out with

#180-grit and finish with #320-grit. Use a sanding block on the lid ends to prevent rounding them over. Put the hinge pins in place in the lids.

Put glue in the mortises and on the surface of the box ends where the front and back parts will contact. Place the tenons on the front and back pieces into the mortises of one end, fit the lids in place, and then slip the other end in place. Getting these parts to align all at the same time can be a challenge.

Using a couple of folded business cards as shims will help to position the lids at the right height as the box is pulled together. Check as the box is clamped together to make certain it is square and that the lids have proper clearance.

## Make the Sliding Tray

The sliding tray for the interior of the box is made using the table saw and a fence clamped at an angle to form the cove. Determining the correct angle for the fence is a trial-and-error process. Raise the height gradually, changing the angle of the fence until you get the cove you want. In order to form a double cove cut with a very slight divider in the middle, I reversed the stock, taking two passes for each change of blade height.

Use a large dowel wrapped in sandpaper to clean up the cove cut. Change grits gradually from coarse to fine. To speed up this operation, a curved scraper can be used.

Put the ³⁄₁₆" straight-cut bit in the router table, and raise the height enough to rout for the dividers in the trays. Slide the tray between stop-blocks to rout for the dividers to fit.

Cut the divider parts to length, then use a ¹⁄₈" roundover bit to shape the ends to fit the routed spaces. Sand the dividers thoroughly before gluing them in place.

Cut the tray ends to length. Rout the inside edges, the top edges and the ends of the tray with a ¹⁄₁₆" roundover bit in the router table.

Sand the end pieces before gluing them in place. Glue the ends of the tray bodies to attach the end pieces, and clamp them in place. To strengthen the joint, drill ¹⁄₈" holes in the ends of the trays for dowels. You can also use a brad nailer to attach the ends.

The tray is shaped by making a series of cuts and using an offset fence clamped to the top of the table saw. Raise the blade in small increments and turn the workpiece end over end as the cove is formed. You can alter the angle of the fence as you go to change the shape and width of cut.

Use a ³⁄₁₆" straight-cut bit in the router table to cut the slots for the tray dividers. Using stops clamped in place on the router table will control the length of cut.

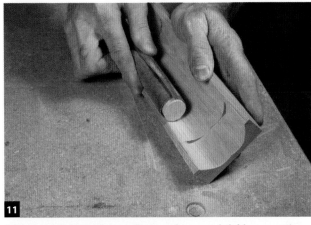

A dowel wrapped in sandpaper will remove the saw marks left by cove cutting.

After assembling the box, use a straight-cut bit in the router table to trim the ends of the tray to fit down over the tray support.

## Make the Pull

The pull is made using the same tenoning techniques as used for the pulls on the winter woods box. Form the tenon on the ends of the pull before it is cut apart.

Form the inner shape with a core box bit; form the outside shape with a chamfering bit. Use the sled on the table saw to finish shaping the tenons.

Hand sand the outside shape of the pull with sandpaper. Use a piece of sandpaper wrapped on a dowel for the inside cove shape.

Apply three coats of Danish oil, and rub with a dry cloth. Glue the pull in place.

**12** Making the pull begins with a cove cut on the router table.

**13** Use a straight-cut router bit to cut the tenon on the end of the pull. After the tenon is formed, the pull can be cut from the walnut stock for further shaping.

# CHAPTER TWENTY

# CHERRY JEWELRY CHEST

Sometimes I find certain boards irresistible, even though I may have no idea right then as to how I'll use the wood. The cherry panel in the top of this box is from such a board. The interesting figuring is from burls forming on the surface of the tree.

This box is made with an unhinged lid that simply pivots and drops into a recess to hold it in the open position, and then closes with a slight lift on the pull, thus eliminating the need for expensive hinges and lid supports. The ebonized walnut pull, the raised trim strip and the feet are chemically treated prior to final assembly to attain their rich black color.

# MATERIALS LIST

| | | |
|---|---|---|
| Sides | 2 | ¾" x 3⁹⁄₁₆" x 11³⁄₁₆" |
| Front | 2 | ¾" x 3⁹⁄₁₆" x 14¹⁄₁₆" |
| Back | 2 | ¾" x 3⁹⁄₁₆" x 14¹⁄₁₆" |
| Bottom | 1 | ¼" x 10" x 13" <br> *Baltic birch plywood* |
| Lid sides | 2 | ⅝" x 1¼" x 9¾" |
| Lid front | 1 | ⅝" x 1¼" x 13⅛" |
| Lid back | 1 | ⅝" x 1¼" x 12¹⁄₁₆" |
| Lid panel | 1 | ⅝" x 8⅛" x 11¹⁄₃₂" |
| Feet | 4 | ¹³⁄₁₆" x 12⁵⁄₁₆" x 8" <br> *Cut to size after gluing* |
| Tray ends | 2 | ⁵⁄₁₆" x 1⅛" x 4⁵⁄₁₆" |
| Tray front | 1 | ⁵⁄₁₆" x 1⅛" x 12¹⁄₁₆" <br> *Includes ⅛" tenons* |
| Tray back | 1 | ⁵⁄₁₆" x 1⅛" x 12¹⁄₁₆" <br> *Includes ⅛" tenons* |
| Tray bottom | 1 | ⅛" x 4¹⁄₁₆" x 12¹⁄₃₂" <br> *Baltic birch plywood* |
| Tray divider | 1 | ⁵⁄₁₆" x ½" x 11¹³⁄₁₆" |
| Tray dividers | 3 or 4 | ⁵⁄₁₆" x ¾" x 3¹³⁄₁₆" |
| Box dividers | 2 | ⁵⁄₁₆" x 1" x 12½" |
| Box dividers | 3 | ⁵⁄₁₆" x 1¼" x 9⅝" |
| Tray guides | 2 | ³⁄₁₆" x ⅜" x 9⅝" |
| Trim strips | 2 | ³⁄₁₆" x ¾" x 27 <br> *Cut to size after ebonizing and finish* |

## Cut the Finger Joints

Set the cut height of the finger joint jig to ⁷⁄₁₆" to allow for a small amount to be sanded flush after assembly. Use a ³⁄₁₆" spiral cutter and cut an index piece to fit over the stop pin. Clamp the index piece in place and make the first cuts in the bottom corners of the end pieces. Then remove the index piece from the jig and make all the cuts in the ends, front and back. Hold the workpiece tight to the pin, stepping over it to align for each consecutive cut. The last cut on each piece will be cut at a miter on the table saw.

Use the miter sled on the table saw to cut the mitered corners at the top of the box. Follow the steps shown in making the bracelet box in chapter sixteen.

Trim the fingers to width on the table saw. Stand the box sides on end and pass them between the saw blade and fence. Set the fence to leave ⁷⁄₁₆", and set the blade to the same height as the router bit in the finger joint jig.

Using the mitered cutoff sled on the table saw, tilt the arbor to 45°. Control the position of the cut with a stop-block, and trim the excess from around the finger joints.

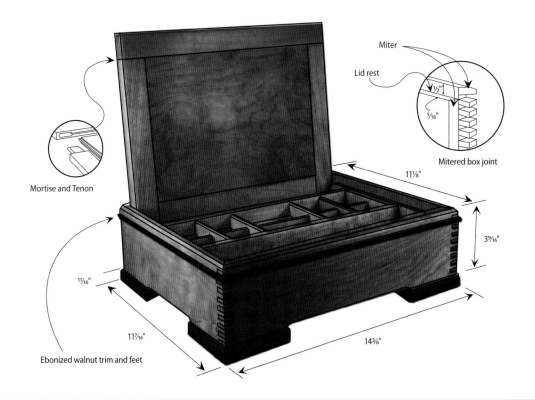

Mortise and Tenon

Miter

Lid rest

½"

⁵⁄₁₆"

Mitered box joint

11⅛"

3⁹⁄₁₆"

1¹⁄₁₆"

11⁷⁄₁₆"

14⅜"

Ebonized walnut trim and feet

Use a template and a pattern maker's bit to rout the clearance in the sides for the lid to open.

Use a squeeze bottle to apply glue to the fingers as the box is assembled.

On the table saw, cut the lip on the box front and sides to provide the frame around the lid. Stand the sides up along the fence to make the first cut, leaving 7/16" remaining of the box side and cutting about 5/8" deep so that the 3/4"-thick lid will stand proud. Next, adjust the fence and saw blade height to cut away the stock from the inside of the front and sides. Perform the same steps on the inside back of the box, but make the first cut 1 3/8" deep to allow for the lid to rest in an open position.

To rout the box sides to provide lid clearance, make a template the same size as the box side from scrap wood. Make a 7/8" x 1 3/8" cut out of one corner, with the 7/8" being measured from the end of the stock. Clamp this template over the box side. With the mortise cleanup bit set to the same depth as the rabbet on the side, rout the recess for the lid.

Before assembly, rout for the box bottom and drawer guides to fit. Sand the inside surfaces of the sides, front, back and bottom. Be sure to check the box for being square as you glue, assemble and clamp it together.

## Make the Lid
Plane or sand the panel to thickness. Use a drum sander to avoid tear-out of the burl pattern.

If the measurements are the same from corner to corner both ways, it is square.

Cut the tenons for the box lid on the table saw.

Use the router table and ¼" straight-cut bit to rout the dados for the top panel to fit.

Use the router table and fence to form the trim strips. Use the 45° chamfering bit first to give it shape, then a straight-cut router bit to cut it to fit the channel in the box.

After cutting the panel frame parts to size, mortise both ends of the front piece and one end on each of the two side pieces with a ¼" straight-cut bit in the router table. Set up stops to control the length of cut, and make the cut to full depth by gradually raising the height of the cutter over a series of steps. Mark a face side on the stock, and make all cuts with the face side against the fence.

Cut the tenons on the back frame piece and on one end of each side piece. First trim the shoulders of the stock, and then using either a tenoning jig on the table saw or a stop-block, stand the pieces on end and shape the tenons. Index each piece with the face side against either the stop-block or the tenoning jig to maintain accuracy.

Use a rasp to trim the shoulders of the tenons to fit the mortises and a chisel to trim in the corners for a final fit.

Test fit the frame parts together. Take careful measurement for cutting the panel to size. Add to the dimensions of the opening ½" in each direction for the ¼" tongues, but subtract about 1/16" in width and about 1/32" in length to allow for wood movement.

With the top frame assembled, use the 45° chamfering bit to rout the inside edges of the frame. Then using a chisel, finish the cut into the corners.

Cut dados in the frame parts for the panel to fit. Rout so that the dados end in the mortises. Stop-blocks can be used, or simply lower the workpiece so the router bit enters the mortise at the opposite end.

Make a relief cut using the table saw, and then, using the 1" straight-cut bit, rout the tongues in the panel edges. Check the fit in the dados cut for the frame.

Use the 45° chamfering bit on edges of the panel where it will intersect the frame. Sand the chamfers on the panel and frame parts. After putting glue into the mortises, assemble the panel and frame and clamp them together. Measure corner to corner on the frame and panel assembly to check for square.

## Make the Trim

Plane some walnut stock down to ⅞" thick and then rip 5/16" strips from it. Use the sanding disc in the table saw to thickness the stock to ¼". Set up the router table and fence with the 45° chamfering bit, and chamfer each edge of the walnut strips. Then change to a straight-cut bit and rout channels in each side of the walnut strips.

Check the thickness of the remaining wood at the center of the strip to see that it measures ⅛".

Sand each edge of the walnut strips, then ebonize them with a vinegar and steel wool solution. When the strips have dried, rub them with steel wool or lightly sand and treat again. Once the strips have reached the desired color, smooth them again with steel wool and finish them with Danish oil.

## Install the Trim

Install a ⅛"bit in the router table, adjusting the fence so that the cut will hit right in the middle of one of the fingers of the finger joints. On my box, I adjusted the fence to measure from the outside of the cut. With the bottom of the box against the fence, rout each side in turn to cut the channel for the trim strips to fit.

On the table saw, cut the individual trim strips. Set the fence so that the tongues remaining on the strips equal the depth of the channels routed for them to fit. In the event that the strips are too tight, widen the distance between the cutter and the fence, and rout the box sides again, slightly widening the channel.

Using the mitered cutoff sled, cut the trim pieces to length. Wait until the body of the box has been sanded and finished with Danish oil before gluing the strips in place.

## Make the Feet

The feet are made using the same techniques used for making the box sides. If you wish to duplicate this box exactly, you will find it helpful to make the feet at the same time as making the box front, back and sides.

After cutting the stock to length, use the box-joint jig and router to cut the finger joints. Follow the same procedure as used for the box sides. Cut the corner stock parts to equal lengths. Plan for some waste when the corners are cut to length. Then cut the inside miters, as with the box sides, and then miter the top corners.

Glue and assemble the sides to form a single unit that will be cut into four corners after the glue has dried. Use the belt and disc sander to clean up the corners, sanding the joints flush.

Use the table saw with the arbor tilted 10° to cut the corners free from the assembled unit. Chamfer the edges, then sand, ebonize and finish with Danish oil

Use the table saw, miter slide and stop-block to shape the pulls. I first trimmed the ends to shape and then the sides.

After tenoning the tray parts, the perfect fit occurs when the parts hold together despite gravity and no glue.

using the same techniques as for making the trim strips. Finally, drill and countersink the bottoms of the feet for attaching to the box.

## Make the Pull

Make the pull from walnut using the same tenoning technique as used for making the pull for the men's jewelry box. Use the table saw with the arbor tilted to

**9**

Use a dado blade in the table saw to cut the lap joints for the divider parts.

pieces moving one direction than the other. This allows for the edges to be routed smooth.

Using a ¼" dado blade and the cutoff sled on the table saw, make a crosscut on a piece of scrap stock. As the scrap stock is milled to thickness, use it to check the thickness of stock for the dividers.

Set the dado blade to half the height of the narrower stock, and clamp a stop-block in place on the sled to locate the position for the dado cut. Change the location of the stop-block to position other cuts, using the same technique to dado the matching pieces.

Rout the edges of the parts prior to assembly with a 45° chamfering bit. This narrows the strips, making them appear thinner. Sand and finish the parts with Danish oil before gluing together.

define its shape. I chose a more geometric shape to go with the inward angle chosen for the feet. Ebonize and finish the pulls to match the feet and trim strips.

## Make the Trays

Mortise the end pieces. Use the same technique on the router table as for the inlaid walnut ring box. Tenon the front and back pieces using the same technique used for making the tenons in the inlaid walnut ring box. The ⅛" mortises and tenons are adequate for this task.

Rout between mortises for the tray bottom to fit. Using a ⅛" kerfed blade in the table saw, cut the dado for the box bottom, so that it will align with the dado cuts in the tray ends.

Using the cutoff sled on the table saw, adjust the blade height to cut through the nubs left on the back and front of the tray. Set the stop-block on the fence to position the cut. Trim the nubs flush with the tenon shoulders. Then rout the edges of the box parts, sand the interior surface and then assemble the trays.

## Make the Dividers

I chose to have removable dividers, which allow the box to be lined before the dividers are put in place. The dividers use a half-overlap system for their parts to be joined and positioned. In order to give a more finished look to the assembled dividers, I use taller stock for the

# CHAPTER TWENTY-ONE

# LUCY'S JEWELRY BOX

My daughter, Lucy, is a box collector. She's saved many old rejected boxes from my workshop scrap pile. It doesn't matter to her whether they are chipped, scratched, broken or still rough unfinished wood. If they're capable of holding some small treasure, they're worth saving. This jewelry box is one I made for her ninth birthday. It is made from pecan and walnut with a small inlaid window of curly maple. It has a drawer at the bottom and an interior tray that lifts as the lid is opened. The pecan was some rough-sawn 5/4 lumber from Texas that a friend sold to me. I was able to resaw it to get ½" planed sides for the box and ⅜" bookmatched panels for the top.

# MATERIALS LIST

| | | |
|---|---|---|
| Front | 1 | ½" x 5½" x 10"<br>*Allows for saw kerf to<br>cut drawer front* |
| Back | 1 | ½" x 5¼" x 10" |
| Sides | 2 | ½" x 5¼" x 8" |
| Top panel | 1 | ½" x 7⅜" x 9⅜"<br>*Includes ³⁄₁₆" tongues<br>on panel* |
| Bottom | 1 | 7⅜" x 9⅜"<br>*⅛" Baltic birch plywood* |
| Dividers | 2 | ³⁄₁₆" x 1¾" x 7¼" |
| Feet | 4 | ½" x 1⅝" 1⅝" |

### Tray

| | | |
|---|---|---|
| Sides | 2 | ⅜" x 1¼" x 4½" |
| Front and back | 2 | ⅜" x 1¼" x 8⅝" |
| Dividers | 2 | ⅛" x ¾" x 4" |
| Bottom | 1 | 4" x 8⅛"<br>*⅛" Baltic birch plywood* |

### Drawer

| | | |
|---|---|---|
| Sides<br>*Includes ³⁄₁₆" tenon* | 2 | ⁵⁄₁₆" x 1¼" x 7⁷⁄₃₂" |
| Back | 1 | ⁵⁄₁₆" x 1¼" x 8¾"<br>*Includes ³⁄₁₆" tenons<br>at each end* |
| Front (cut from front of box) | | ½" x 1¼" x 10" |
| Bottom | 1 | ⅛" x 6¹⁵⁄₁₆" x 8⅝"<br>*Baltic birch plywood* |

### Tray Lift Mechanism

| | | |
|---|---|---|
| Front lift arms | 2 | ³⁄₁₆" x ½" x 2½" |
| Back lift arms | 2 | ³⁄₁₆" x ½" x 4½"<br>*From ¹⁄₁₆" brass sheet<br>stock* |
| Screws and nuts | 2 | 8nc32 x ½" long<br>*Flat head brass* |
| Brass screws | 8 | #4 x ½" long<br>*Flat head* |

### Hardware and Supplies

| | | |
|---|---|---|
| Screws | 6 | 1¼" #6<br>*Flat head* |
| Curly maple and walnut stock for inlay | | |
| ⅛" walnut stock for trim | | |
| ⅛" x ½" walnut stock for slip feathers | | |
| ⁵⁄₁₆" x 1¼" walnut stock for drawer pulls | | |

## Overview

This is one of the more complicated boxes in the book and one that I suggest for more advanced woodworkers who may already have some understanding of the sequence of steps required. Many of the techniques used are covered in other projects. The following is an overview of making Lucy's jewelry box, with some of the steps left out because of space requirements.

## Making the Box

After planing the material to thickness, rip the stock to width, leaving it wide enough to allow for the saw-kerf width that will be required for cutting the drawer apart from the front. Select the piece of wood that will be the

To make efficient use of material, resaw the material for the sides from thicker stock. This process also gives better opportunity to match grains and color of wood.

Use the miter sled on the table saw to cut the miters at the corners of the box. Use a stop-block clamped to the fence to control the lengths of the parts.

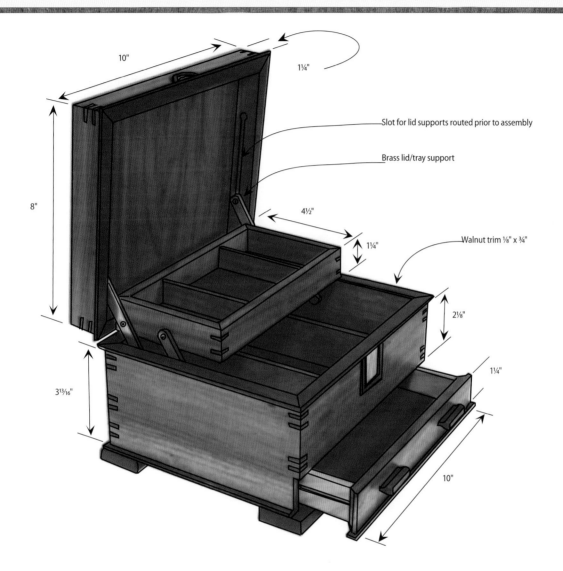

10"

1¼"

8"

Slot for lid supports routed prior to assembly

Brass lid/tray support

4½"

1¼"

Walnut trim ⅛" x ¾"

2⅛"

3¹³⁄₁₆"

1¼"

10"

front of the box, and cut away the lower portion. This lower portion will become the drawer front. Use the table saw to cut the dados in the front, back and sides to allow for the top panel, box bottom and drawer guides.

Tilt the saw arbor to 45° and use the 45°-angled sled to cut the box sides, front and back to the required lengths. Rip saw the box sides, front and back to about ⅟₃₂" over finished dimension, and then use the jointer to bring the parts to finished size.

With a ³⁄₁₆" bit in the router table, and using stop-blocks to control the movement of the box front and back along the fence, rout for the interior dividers to fit. Use the table saw to cut away the front lower portions of the box sides where the drawer front will fit.

**3**

Build a model of the tray lift mechanism. This will help you understand the relationship between parts and will be useful in setting up to mill the actual parts.

Use a key-hole router bit to rout in the box side for the tray lift mechanism to fit, using the parts from the model as a guide for setup.

Use the model for setting up to drill the box sides for the lift mechanism to fit. This needs to be done before the box is assembled.

Use the router table to cut the tongues on the panel top. Note the relief cut made on the table saw prior to routing. Use a 1" straight-cut router bit, and clamp safety blocking securely in place to protect your fingers.

## Make the Tray Lifters and Lid Supports

In making this box, it's helpful to create a working model of the relationships between parts to help locate the exact positions for holes to be drilled and slots to be cut. I made my model from bits and pieces of scrap Masonite. In making the model, the parts should be sized to correspond to the end view of the lid and box sides after the saw-kerf is subtracted in separating the lid from the base. Also allow for the ⅛" walnut bandings that will be added to the edges.

Using a keyhole bit, rout in the box side for the screw to attach the lift mechanism. Use the fence and stop-blocks to control the length and position of the cut. Use the model to determine the locations inside the box for the mechanism to fit, and drill the pilot holes before the box is assembled.

Make the small lift parts using the model to determine the lengths. Make the rear lifters from three layers of sheet brass. Use an old carbide blade in the table saw to cut the brass, then round the corners on a belt sander before polishing.

## Make the Panel Top

Resaw enough pecan to form the top panel and plane it to thickness. Joint and glue the panels to achieve the full width required (it's good to make a relief cut with the table saw to ease the router's work by reducing the router's pull on the workpiece). After forming the panel, use a ¹⁄₁₆" roundover bit to shape its edge and to soften the edge of the box sides where the panel will intersect.

## Assemble the Box

After sanding the inside surfaces of the box sides, front, back, top panel, bottom and dividers, apply glue to the mitered surfaces and use band clamps to hold the miters closed tightly until the glue sets. Be sure to put the internal dividers in place as the box is assembled. Use a spacer block at the bottom front of the box to keep the box from squeezing in where the drawer will fit. After the glue has fully dried, use the slip-feather jig on the router table to cut for the walnut corner splines to fit. Place the walnut slip feathers into the corners using glue to lock them in place. Sand the splines flush with the surrounding surface of the box.

7

Use a ⅛" roundover bit in the router table to shape the edges of the panel. I raise the height of the router bit above the table to allow for the tongue on the panel. Lower the bit before routing the matching roundover on the inside edges of the box sides.

## Make the Inlay Templates

Making and inlaying the parts for the front of the box requires making three templates and using the inlay guide bushing set used for the wedding ring music box. The primary template is used to form the working templates for shaping and inlaying the parts.

First, drill a hole in plywood stock the same size as the box front for ease of alignment when installing the inlay. Drill a hole larger than the planned inlay, and using the table saw, cut into the circle from the edge of the stock to form the oblong squared shape. Replace the lower portion of the cut with a piece of plywood to close the shape, and attach these with brads to a second piece of plywood of the same size.

Place the template and the shape beneath it over a template-following bit in your router table. Following the guide bearing, cut the shape of the first working template in the template stock. Separate the template from the initial forms and attach the new working template to another piece of plywood of the same size. Then using the inlay guide bushing set, rout the second template using the first working template to determine its shape and size. Using the guide bushing set creates a second template smaller in size than the original.

8

Spread glue on the miters before assembly. The raised panel should not be glued in place.

9

Use band clamps to hold the box parts in position as the glue sets. Check that the box is square before the glue dries. This can be done either with a small square or by measuring from corner to corner.

10

Use the slip-feather jig on the router table to cut the box corners for the slip feathers to fit. The block of wood resting in the V positions the cut.

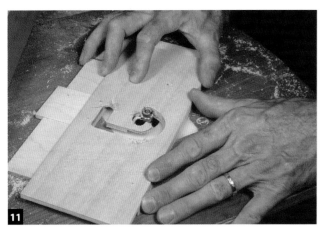

**11** Use the mortise cleanup router bit in the router table to form the template for inlaying the front of the box. The underlying template used to guide the cut is made by drilling a hole in a piece of plywood, cutting into it from the edge using the table saw, then nailing this piece and a small filler block in place on the workpiece.

**12** Use the first template to guide in making the second. Using the inlay guide bushing set with the brass bushing in place creates an offset template smaller than the first.

**13** Use the larger template to rout the front of the box for the inlay to fit. Start by lowering the cutter into the stock, then follow the perimeter of the template before removing the waste.

**14** Use these two templates to cut the parts for inlay. I use carpet tape to adhere the inlay stock to a piece of scrap wood, then clamp the template in place. Inside shapes are routed with the brass bushing in place. Outside shapes are routed with the brass bushing removed.

## Inlay the Front

This procedure is the same as used for making the triangle ring box except that the templates are clamped in place. Clamp the first template in place over the front of the box. Then use the router, ⅛" router bit and guide bushing with the brass bushing in place. Set the depth of cut to about ¹⁄₁₆". Test on a piece of scrap, and use the dial caliper to check depth. Remove all the material inside the space defined by the template with your router.

Remove the brass bushing and adjust the depth of cut. Then clamp the template in place over a piece of walnut. Use double-stick carpet tape to firmly attach the walnut to some scrap stock so it doesn't shift during the routing operations.

Install the brass bushing to the guide bushing. Clamp the template with the smaller opening over the walnut stock and rout to cut away the inside of the piece. Clamp the smaller template over a piece of curly

15

After the inlay space is defined on the box, use the table saw to cut the lid from the body of the box. Use shims to keep the box parts in position so they will not bind on the blade.

16

Use the router table with fence and ³⁄₁₆" straight-cut router bit to cut the mortises in the drawer sides and front. Move the workpiece between the stops clamped to the fence.

17

Cut the tenons for the drawer sides and back on the router table with a 1" straight-cut router bit.

maple taped to scrap stock. After removing the bushing, rout the maple piece.

Rout the edges of the walnut piece and hand sand it to prepare it for inlaying. Cut the inlay pieces apart and glue them in place after the lid is cut from the box. Use the table saw to cut the lid away from the base of the box, replacing the saw-kerf with shims to keep the box from closing on the blade.

## Make the Drawer

The drawers are made using mortise-and-tenon joints like when making the inlaid ring box. First, cut the drawer to fit the shape of the front of the box. Use the ⅛" router bit in the router table to rout mortises in the drawer front for the sides to fit. Change the position of the fence and stops to rout mortises into the drawer sides for the tenons on the drawer back to fit.

With a 1" straight-cut bit, rout tenons on the drawer back and sides. Check the fits in the mortise and adjust if necessary.

Using the sled on the table saw, trim nubs from the tenons to make them the same width as the mortises. Rout the sides, front and back for the drawer bottom to fit. Rout for the drawer pulls to fit. Prior to assembly,

cut the drawer face to match the shape of the box front using the miter cutoff sled.

## Make the Drawer Pulls

Unlike the pull used in the men's jewelry box, the drawer pulls used here are routed with a roundover bit for their final shaping rather than a chamfering bit (see

18

After trimming the tenons to width using the table saw sled, the drawer can be trial-assembled.

19

Use the miter sled to trim the drawer front to fit the sides of the box. The stop-block controls the position of the cut and the blade height is lowered to allow for the overlap at the front of the box.

20

Use the router table to cut the mortises in the tray front and back for dividers to fit. I use a ⅛" straight-cut router bit. Note the dado cut for the tray bottom to fit.

the instructions for making the men's jewelry box for the proper technique).

## Make the Tray

Cut the miters for the tray using the miter cutoff sled on the table saw. Then before assembly, rout the slots for the dividers and for the tray bottom to fit. Apply glue to the corners and fit the dividers and bottom in place as the tray is assembled. Use the slip-feather jig on the router table to rout for the slip feathers to fit.

## Attach the Walnut Trim

Hand sand the inlay parts before fitting them into the box front. They should be sanded before the final cutting and gluing. Use a brad nailer and glue to attach the walnut trim strips. Miter them to fit the corners, and carefully fit them to the bottom of the drawer front and bottom of the box. Cut walnut feet and attach them with wood screws and clear adhesive. You will need to cut a small relief space on the front feet to provide clearance for the drawer to slide without scraping.

As with all the other boxes, sand through a range of grits up to about #320-grit and then use Danish oil to finish. After oiling, install the interior tray, lift mechanism and lid support. To attach it to the lid, use a flathead brass screw and nut tapped into the brass lift mechanism.

**21**

Hand sand the inlay parts before final fitting to the box lid and body. Use the table saw and sled to cut the parts to final size.

**22**

Miter the walnut trim pieces to fit the lid and box body. I use a brad nailer and glue to attach the trim strips.

**23**

Use a tap to cut threads in the brass supports to hold the screws in place.

**24**

Check the operation of the tray lift before installing the lid (one brass support arm will have to be removed and replaced as the lid is attached).

# CHAPTER TWENTY-TWO

# ASH CHEST OF DRAWERS

This chest of drawers is made with wood originally harvested from the White River Valley in northwest Arkansas as Beaver Lake was constructed by the U.S. Army Corps of Engineers in the 1950s. The densely figured wood was then used as a kitchen countertop in my home. After nearly 20 years of use, the 2½" slab of solid ash had badly warped. When we replaced the countertop, the thick slab of ash was put away in my shop while my imagination was stirring. How could I make use of this beautiful piece of wood? Now in the wood's new life, it is a box. Remember the stories your wood can tell, and become a storyteller through your woodworking!

# MATERIALS LIST

| | | | |
|---|---|---|---|
| Top and bottom | 2 | | ⅞" x 7¾" x 9"<br>*Cut smaller after<br>mortises are cut* |
| Sides | 2 | | 1¹⁄₁₆" x 5¾" x 8¼"<br>*Length includes ¼"<br>tenons* |
| Back panel | 1 | | ⅜" x 6" x 8⅛" |
| ***Drawer Parts*** | | | |
| Fronts | 5 | | ⅜" x 1½" x 7½" |
| Sides | 10 | | ⅜" x 1½" x 5⁹⁄₁₆"<br>*Includes ³⁄₁₆" tenon* |
| Backs | 5 | | ⅜" 1½" x 5¼"<br>*Includes ³⁄₁₆" tenons* |
| Drawer guides | 10 | | ³⁄₁₆" x ⁵⁄₁₆" x 5⁵⁄₁₆" |
| Drawer pulls | 5 | | ⁵⁄₁₆" x 1¼" x 2"<br>*Cut from walnut stock* |

## Construction Notes

I resawed 2¼" solid stock into halves each 1⅛" thick. You will need 5/4 stock to make this box or adjust the sides and bottom to use narrower stock and change the angle of the sides.

## Make the Carcass

Rout the mortises in the top and bottom of the box. Use the router table and ³⁄₁₆" spiral cutter to rout the mortises to a ¼" depth. Use stop-blocks clamped to the fence to control the lengths of the mortises, and check their depth with a dial caliper. As a variation, you could also build this piece using a biscuit joiner #20 biscuits.

Cut the tenons on the box sides. Because of the amount of material that must be removed, it is safest to do this job on the table saw. Fit the tenon into the mortise to

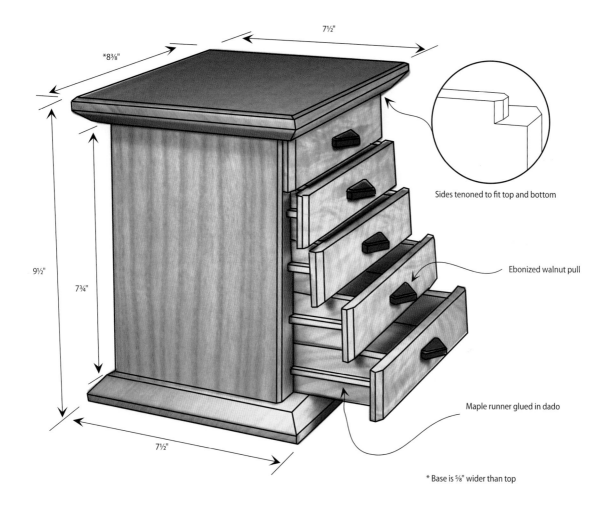

Sides tenoned to fit top and bottom

Ebonized walnut pull

Maple runner glued in dado

7½"

*8⅜"

9½"

7¾"

7½"

* Base is ⅝" wider than top

Use a ¹⁄₁₆" straight-cut bit to cut the top and bottom mortises. With stops clamped to the fence to control the length of the mortises, lower the workpiece over the moving bit and move it between stops.

Using the table saw, begin cutting the tenons on the box sides. The first cut is made with the workpiece flat on the table saw.

Adjust the height of cut and position of the table saw fence to finish cutting the tenons. I prefer to cut a test piece first to check for an accurate fit in the mortises.

After forming the tenons on the box sides and trimming the tenons to width, draw a line to follow on the band saw, tapering the box sides. The exact angle is not critical to the design, but both sides should match.

check the fit (it's helpful to use a test piece to check the fit before cutting the real thing).

With a straight rule, mark the angle on the sides. Then with the band saw, cut the sides to shape.

Rout the sides for the back panel to fit. Use the ³⁄₁₆" bit in the router table and raise the bit to ¼" height above the table. Then change the fence location, and rout the top and bottom for the back panel to fit.

With a ³⁄₁₆" bit, rout the drawer guide channels in the box sides. Use stop-blocks to prevent routing through the dado for holding the back panel in place. Make the back panel using the same technique used in making the top panel for Lucy's jewelry box. Then cut the top to size, trimming from each end.

With a 45° chamfering bit, rout the profile of the base, and the front and back of the top (the ends need to be cut on the table saw). Hand-sanding the base and top will keep the edges crisp.

## Assembly

Sand all the parts of the box carcass prior to assembly. Then with a squeeze bottle, apply glue to the inside of the mortises before assembly, but don't glue the back panel in place, as it needs to be left free to expand and contract. With several clamps, hold the chest together as the glue dries. Scrap hardboard between the clamps and the chest itself will prevent marring the surfaces.

Reduce the proportion of the box top by cutting on the sled with the stop-block. This must be done after the mortises are cut. Reducing the size of the top keeps the box from feeling top heavy.

Use a sanding block to sand the chamfers to keep the edges crisp. By using a series of sanding grits, the hand sanding goes very quickly.

Use a 45° chamfering bit to rout the front edge of the chest top, but use the table saw at an angle to shape the ends.

Rout the drawer sides with the ³⁄₁₆" straight-cut bit for the drawer guides to fit. Check the fit of the drawers one at a time, and adjust the dado for the drawer guides as needed for proper clearance before the drawers are assembled.

Sand the inside of the drawer front, and the inside and outside of the drawer sides, back and bottom. Assemble them with glue in the mortises, then clamp them together with bar clamps, checking to make certain they are square.

Cut ³⁄₁₆" x ³⁄₈" strips to use as drawer guides. With a ³⁄₁₆" bit, rout the drawer sides for the drawer guides to fit. Routing test pieces will help in aligning the drawers to fit.

Before cutting the drawer fronts to length and angle to match the cabinet sides, rout for the drawer pulls to fit. Then after putting the drawer in place in the cabinet, use a pencil to mark the position of the cabinet side on the back of the drawer front. With the sled on the table saw, use blocking to set up the angle of cut. Align the pencil mark with the far side of the saw-kerf so that the drawers will be ⅛" narrower than the total width of the chest.

## Make the Drawers

Each of the drawers is the same width, although they appear to taper along with the shape of the cabinet. To build the drawers, first resaw the material for drawer fronts, backs and sides (I used ash for the interior drawer parts). After cutting the parts to length, rout the mortises in the box sides and front. Follow the same procedure you used in making the box ends for the inlaid walnut ring box.

Using the router table and fence with a 1" straight-cut bit, cut the tenons at the ends of the box back and sides to fit the mortises. Rout the fronts, backs and sides for the box bottoms to fit. Set the ⅛" bit to a ⅛" height, ⅛" from the fence.

## Finish the Chest

Make your drawer pulls. The triangle shape that I used is designed to go with the angular shape of the jewelry chest. Finally, use Danish oil to finish all the parts and bring out the rich warm color of the natural wood.

8

9

In fitting the drawer sides, work from the bottom up, carefully measuring and adjusting the router table fence as needed to cut the channels for the drawer guides to fit. Glue the drawer guides to the drawers after fitting is complete.

Starting at the top of the chest, mark the drawers for cutting to width and angle to conform to the sides of the chest.

10

11

Use simple tacked-in-place strips on the sled to position the drawers at the right angle. The two strips are at opposing angles for cutting the opposite sides of the drawer.

Use the sled to cut the drawer pulls to shape after the tenons are formed. The small clamp and stop-blocks hold the pull safely, allowing the fingers to be well out of the way of the saw blade.

# CHAPTER TWENTY-THREE

# TRIANGLE TOWER

Many of my designs start as mere basic sketches, with many of the details unresolved, as I find it easier to assemble elements of a design and then play with the parts to develop the finished concept. This project changed several times as it evolved and took almost a year of play to reach its finished form. The triangular trays are made of sassafras, with walnut splines, or slip feathers, joining the corners. The trays pivot on a brass welding rod, swinging forward to reveal their contents. It is a challenge to a person's self-confidence to embark on a project not knowing exactly how it will look when completed. Taking risks in design often leads to failure. But without the willingness to risk failure, new things would never be created.

# MATERIALS LIST

| | | |
|---|---|---|
| Bottom trays | 6 | $5/16$" x $1\frac{3}{4}$" x $5^{15}/16$" |
| Middle trays | 24 | $5/16$" x $1\frac{1}{4}$" x $5^{15}/16$" |
| Top trays | 6 | $5/16$" x $1\frac{1}{8}$" x $5^{15}/16$" |
| Corner triangles | 12 | $\frac{3}{4}$" long<br>*Make from $^{11}/16$ stock* |
| Bottoms | 12 | $5\frac{5}{8}$" on long side<br>*Size is prior to final shaping. Cut from $\frac{1}{8}$" x 4"-wide Baltic birch. Final shape requires template routing.* |
| Base | 4 | 1" x $1\frac{7}{8}$" x $8\frac{5}{8}$"<br>*Cut angle 30° at one end, 60° at other* |
| Panel | 1 | $\frac{1}{8}$" Baltic Birch<br>*Cut from stock 6" x 10" x $\frac{1}{2}$"* |
| Top | 1 | $\frac{7}{8}$" x $7\frac{1}{2}$" x $13\frac{1}{4}$"<br>*Cut as shown in technical art* |
| Vertical stretchers | 2 | 1" x $1\frac{3}{4}$" x $9\frac{1}{2}$"<br>*Includes $\frac{5}{8}$"-long tenons and each end* |
| **Hardware** | | |
| Hinge rods | 2 | $3/16$" dia. x $9\frac{1}{2}$"<br>*Make from brass welding rod* |
| Steel washers | 14 | $\frac{1}{4}$"<br>*Paint black* |
| Wood screws | 4 | #6 x $1\frac{5}{8}$" long<br>*Flat head* |

## Make the Triangles

After planing the tray side stock to its finished size, cut the parts to length using the adjustable sled in the table saw. The stop-block clamped in position insures uniform length of the parts. Then glue the sides together to make the triangles, using rubber bands to hold the sides together as the glue dries.

Use the slip-feather jig on the router table to cut for the walnut splines to fit. Make a sliding tray at the correct angle to hold the corners as they are routed.

Cut triangle wedges to fit the slots, and glue them in place. Then sand the outside surfaces of the triangle trays so that the wedges are flush.

Glue the corner blocks in place. Note the V-block used to protect the tip of the triangle from clamping pressure. With a drill press, drill the corners for the $3/16$" brass rod to fit.

Rout the recess for the box bottom to fit, using a rabbeting bit. I used a rabbeting set that includes an oversized bearing to allow the very small cut required.

Shape the box bottoms with a template-following router bit. Use a simple frame to hold the bottom panel and template together for routing.

**1**

Clamp the box sides firmly in place as they are cut to length. Use a sled, adjustable fence, stop-block and a C-clamp.

**2**

Spread glue on the corners.

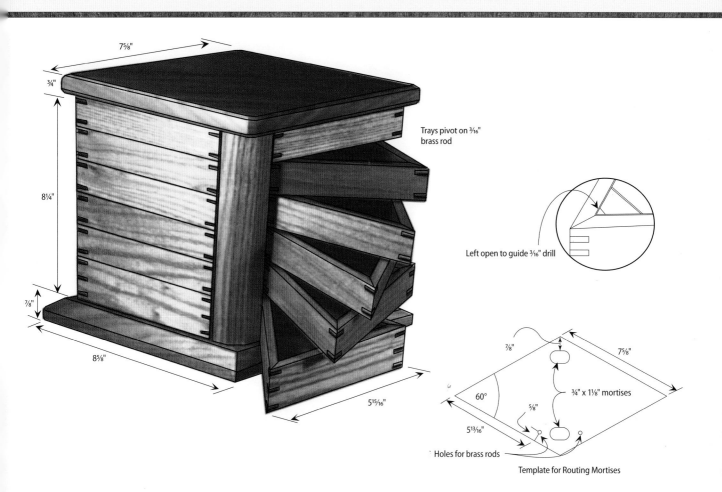

7⅝"

¾"

8¼"

⅞"

8⅝"

5¹⁵⁄₁₆"

Trays pivot on ³⁄₁₆"
brass rod

Left open to guide ³⁄₁₆" drill

⅞"

7⅝"

60°

¾" x 1⅛" mortises

⅝"

5¹³⁄₁₆"

Holes for brass rods

Template for Routing Mortises

**3**

Use rubber bands to hold the parts securely as the glue sets.

**4**

Use the slip-feather jig on the router table to cut for the slip feathers to fit. The length of the dowel between the workpiece and the fence will position the cut. For subsequent cuts, the dowel can be cut shorter.

**5** Use the sled to cut the small slip feathers from solid stock. Turn the walnut stock over between each cut. The push stick keeps the fingers safely away from the blade.

**6** With glue spread in the slot and on the slip feathers, slip them in place.

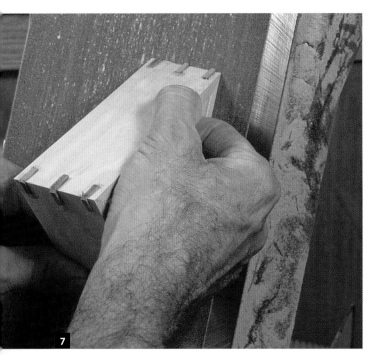

**7** Use the 6" x 48" belt sander to sand the slip feathers flush with the sides.

**8** Cut corner blocks for the triangle drawer units. Use a fence and stop-block on the table saw fence and a push stick.

9

Use V-blocks and C-clamps to glue the corner blocks in place. Carefully align the edges as the parts are assembled.

11

Use a pilot-point router bit to cut the ¼"-wide by ⅛"-deep rabbets for the tray bottoms to fit.

10

Drill for the pivot rod to fit the triangle trays. Leave a slight space in the corner so that when the corner block is fitted, a natural point of travel is allowed for the drill bit to keep it from wandering.

12

Shape a template piece to fit the tray bottom, then use it as a guide for shaping the box bottoms. The V-block holds the pieces in alignment with the template without clamping.

## Make the Base

The base is constructed of four pieces of 2"-wide sassafras stock and uses the bottom panel as a spline connecting the parts. As in cutting the parts for the triangle trays, use the adjustable angle sled to cut the parts to size (you'll need to change the angle to cut the opposite ends to length).

Use a ⅛"-kerf saw blade and with the blade height raised to about 1½", stand the bottom parts on edge along the fence and cut for the bottom panel to fit. Use the sled to cut the bottom panels to size.

Rout and sand the inside edges of the sassafras parts and the bottom panel prior to gluing. Then squeeze glue

13

To make the base for the triangle tower, cut parts to shape and use a chamfering bit to shape the inside edges. The ⅛" birch plywood bottom also serves as a spline holding the sides together. Spread glue on the ends and use a band clamp to hold the parts together while the glue dries.

14

Use a template-following mortise cleanup bit to cut the mortises in the bottom and top of the triangle tower. Clamp the template in place and then, using a plunge router, gradually lower the cutter into the work piece.

into the saw-kerf and assemble the parts around the bottom panel. Use a band clamp to hold the parts in alignment as the glue sets.

## Make the Tower Top

Cut and plane sassafras stock to oversize dimension, and then using the angle sled on the table saw, trim the top piece to size. At the same time, cut a template piece to size from scrap plywood. This will be used for routing the mortises into the top and bottom of the cabinet.

With a plunge router and a ⅝" straight-cut bit, rout the locations for the mortises in the plywood template according to the measurements given in the drawing. Clamp the template to the top of the underside of the tower. Using the ½" mortise cleanup bit in the plunge router, rout the mortises for the-vertical stretchers to-fit to a depth of about ⅝".

Position the template on the base and rout the mortises in it. Turn the template over between routing the top and the bottom to make sure the bottom is the mirror linage of the top. To accommodate the brass rods, drill the ³⁄₁₆" holes into the top. Drill the same holes in the template and then use the template to mark and drill the holes in the bottom.

## Make the Vertical Stretchers

Measure the heights of the trays including the washers used as spacers between them. Also measure the heights of the top and bottom. Cut the vertical stretchers to that length plus 1¼" for the two ⅝" tenons to fit the top and bottom.

Cut tenons on the ends of the vertical stretchers using the table saw and the sled or the tenoning jig. Use a rasp to then round the corners of the tenons. To ease the process, you can also use a band saw to cut 45° shoulders from the tenons.

The vertical stretcher at the front will have to be routed to provide clearance for the trays to pivot when opened. Use a core-box bit in the router table to form the curved portion of the clearance. Then use the table saw to finish the cut. Rout the remaining edges with a chamfering bit.

## Assemble the Triangle Tower

Cut the brass rod to length, then bevel the ends on the belt and disc sander. Rout the edges of the top, bottom

**15** With pivot pin holes drilled in the template, and with the vertical stretchers in place, mark the locations for the pivot holes in the base and top of the triangle tower.

and vertical stretchers with a chamfering bit. Sand all the parts starting with #150-grit and finishing with #320. Glue the tray bottoms in place, and then use Danish oil to finish all the parts.

Align the trays along the brass rods using the brass washers between trays. After spreading glue in the mortises, assemble the triangle towers and clamp them together until the glue dries.

With a template the same size and shape as the inside or the trays, use a rotary cutter to cut the lining material to size and glue them in place with white glue.

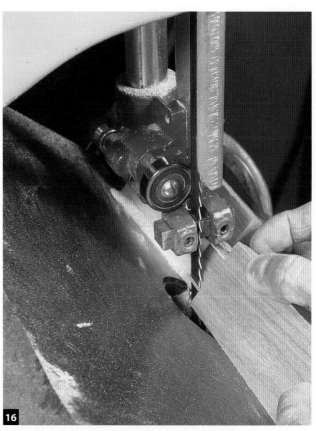

**16** After cutting the tenons on the table saw, use the band saw with its table at a 45° angle to trim the corners of the tenons prior to rasping.

**17** As the triangle tower is assembled, use paste wax to lubricate the pivot rod. Place washers between the parts to provide clearance for opening.

# CHAPTER TWENTY-FOUR

# TRIBUTE TO AMERICAN LINDEN

I believe the job of an artist is to use his or her tools of expression to help others connect with the world. We often discover value in things only after they have been pointed out to us as having value. This box is intended as my tribute to American linden, commonly known as basswood. While technically a hardwood, it is softer than many softwoods and takes carving details easily. My wood carving skills are somewhat limited. But by using skills both inherent and learned, I can express what is important in my life, telling a story in the process. And the stories we tell with our woodworking express our innermost values more powerfully and sincerely than words alone.

## MATERIALS LIST

| | | |
|---|---|---|
| Sides | 2 | 3/4" x 8" x 9 1/16" |
| Front | 1 | 3/4" x 8 1/4" x 12 1/16" *Before cutting of drawer fronts* |
| Top panel | 1 | 1/2" x 8 1/16" x 11 1/16" |
| Bottom | 1 | 1/4" x 8 1/16" x 1 1/16" *Baltic birch plywood* |
| Dividers | 3 | 1/4" x 3/4" x 10 1/4" |
| Dividers | 2 | 1/4" x 7/8" x 7 9/16" |
| Base | 2 | 7/8" x 1 5/8" x 13 1/2" |
| Base | 2 | 7/8" x 1 8/8" x 10 1/2" |
| Bottom | 1 | 1/8" x 9 1/8" x 12 1/8" *Baltic birch plywood* |
| Back | 1 | 3/4" x 8" x 12 1/16" |
| ***Upper Drawers*** | | |
| Facings | 2 | 3/4" x 1 1/2" x 12" |
| Sides | 4 | 7/16" x 1 1/2" x 7 13/16" *Includes 1/4" tenon* |
| Backs | 2 | 7/16" x 1 1/2" x 10 1/16" *Includes 1/4" tenons* |
| Bottoms | 2 | 1/4" x 7 1/2" x 10" *Baltic birch plywood* |
| Dividers | 4 | 1/4" x 7/8" x 9 9/16" |
| Dividers | 4 | 1/4" x 1 1/8" x 7 1/8" |
| ***Lower Drawer*** | | |
| Facing | 1 | 3/4" x 1 15/16" x 12" |
| Sides | 2 | 7/16" x 1 15/16" x 7 13/16" *Includes 1/4" tenon* |
| Back | 1 | 7/16" x 1 15/16" x 10 1/16" *Includes 1/4" tenons* |
| Bottom | 1 | 1/4" x 7 3/16" x 10 1/16" *Baltic birch plywood* |
| ***Hardware*** | | |
| Pulls | 6 | 3/16" x 1/2" x 1 3/4" |
| Quadrant hinges | 1 pr. | |
| Flathead screws | 6 | #6 x 1 5/8" |

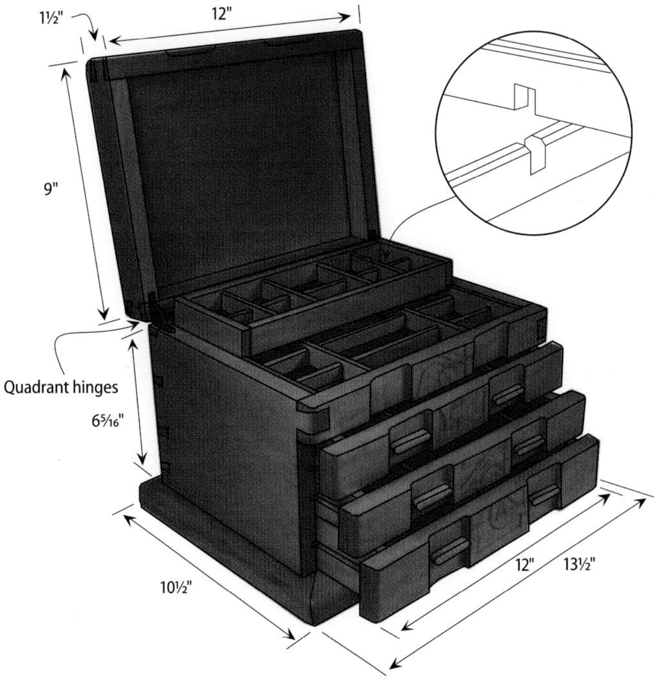


## Making the Box

This project is made with hand-cut dovetails and carved with a simple relief pattern of leaves, twigs and fruit modeled after the simple line drawings in one of my favorite books, "Trees of Arkansas" by Dwight Moore. In selecting the parts for this box, I wanted the front to be from a single board and matched to the sides and back. I therefore used stock wide enough to allow for the saw-kerfs when cutting and separating the drawers.

## Shape the Front of the Box

Make a template for routing the recess that will not only house the pulls, but also define the areas for carving and provide the lift area for the lid. Use scrap material to build the form by overlapping and nailing corners.

Clamp the template in place. Using a bowl-cutting bit with a guide bearing, rout the recess at one side.

**Use a simple template and bowl-cutting router bit to form the shape of the front of the chest.**

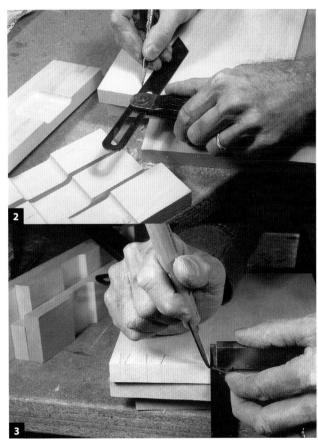

2

3

Use a sliding T-bevel, a marking gauge and a square to lay out the dovetails. Note that the drawer front parts have been ripped from the other portion of the front of the chest.

Change the location of the template, and rout the other side. Sand the interior spaces of the shaped areas. Then cut the drawer fronts from the box front stock, leaving the box front remaining.

## Joint the Corners

When cutting the dovetails, some craftsmen prefer to cut the pins first and then the tails; others like me, do the opposite. Mark out the location of the tails using a sliding T-bevel, a small square, a pencil and a marking gauge.

For cutting the tails, my preference is to use a Japanese dozuki saw, whose teeth cut on the pull rather than the push. When laying out the tails, be careful to allow for the saw-kerf, which will be cut away when separating the lid from the body of the box.

Chisel the waste from between the tails. American linden is very soft and easy to chisel. To keep the edges crisp and clean, make your first cuts away from the marking gauge lines, and then when most of the stock has been removed, align the chisel with the marked lines to make the final cuts.

Use the cut tails to mark where the pins will be cut. I use a small chip-carving knife rather than a pencil because the cut line conforms more closely to the shape of the tails. Place the tailed stock in position over the

4

Use a sharp chisel to remove the waste between the dovetails.

5

Use a chisel to clean up the sides of the tails. I do this to square the edges and remove the saw marks.

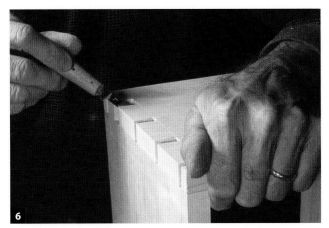

6

Use a sharp knife to mark the shape of the pins directly from the cut tails.

7

Use a chisel to remove the waste between the pins. Make your final shearing cut by using the marking gauge scored line to position the chisel.

8

Use the router table and straight-cut router bit to cut the dados for the drawer guides, top panel and chest bottom to fit. Adjust the fence to position the cuts and use stop-blocks clamped to the table to control the length of the cuts so as not to appear on the outside of the chest.

9

After cutting the mitered corners, check the fit of the pins and tails.

end of the pin stock, and trace the shape of the tails with the knife. Use the dozuki saw to cut the shape of the pins, and chisel away the remaining waste. Cut only the inside portion of the top tails, leaving some to be cut away for the mitered corners. I don't spend enough time cutting dovetails to be perfect at it, and I always seem to spend some time monkeying with the final fit.

Use the 45° sled on the table saw to cut the miters in the top corners. Cut the box sides to allow for the drawers to fit with the table saw, but be careful not to cut all the way through. Finish the cut with the dozuki saw

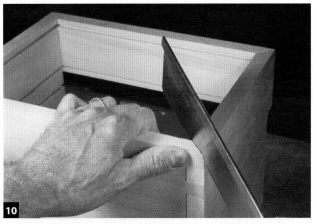

10

With the corners pulled almost closed, use the dozuki saw to clean up the mitered cut. The dovetail joint should be open about a saw-kerf wide to bring a perfect fit.

Use cutout shapes to design the carved pattern. The heart shape of the American linden leaves makes them appealing for a jewelry box without being trite.

Do the carving on the front of the box using a small straight chisel and shallow gouge. I follow the pencil outlines with the straight chisel and then remove the waste between with the gouge.

The paper template bends easily to carry the design up and over the front edge of the box and onto the top.

and chisel it smooth by holding the chisel flat against the sawn surface.

With the router table fence and a ¼" straight-cut bit, rout the box sides for the drawer guides to fit. Use the dozuki saw to finish fit the miters at the box corners.

## Make and Fit the Top Panel and Box Bottom

Measure the inside space into which the top will fit, then add ½" to each dimension, reduce the length by $\frac{1}{32}$" and the width by $\frac{1}{16}$" to allow for clearance, expansion and contraction. Cut the top panel and box bottom to these dimensions.

Rout channels for the top and bottom to fit. Use stops positioned along the router table fence to keep the cut from exiting the workpieces. Then with the table saw, define the tongues on the top panel.

## Assembly

Before assembling the box, sand all inside surfaces. Spread glue on the surfaces of the tails and pins where they will meet. Carefully pull the parts into position and clamp if necessary. Check to make sure the box carcass is square. When the glue has dried, sand the dovetails and pins flush with the surrounding wood, and use a ½"-radius roundover bit to give the top corners of the box its finished shape.

## Carve the Design

When laying out the design, remember to allow for the saw-kerf when the box top is removed from the body. I started my carving on the box before it was assembled to keep from hammering too much on the assembled box. Position the various drawer fronts and the box front in order so the sketch of the carving will cover all the parts. I use cut-out shapes of leaves to achieve a pattern. The leaves can be folded and traced to form different shapes and changed in size and orientation to create a pleasing design. Use a pencil to sketch in the branches (pencil lines can be erased easily from the basswood, so play with the design until you find one that you like). Remember skill in design is like every other thing you will learn in woodworking; it will evolve with time and experience. You may find it easier to develop a design for carving from a line drawing than from a photograph,

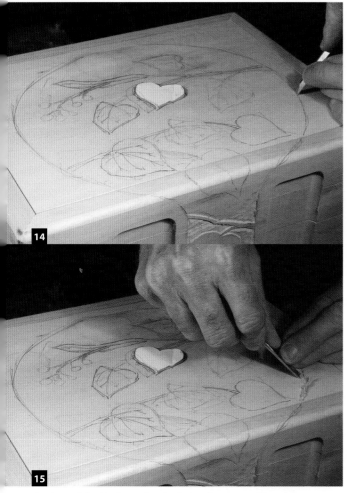

14

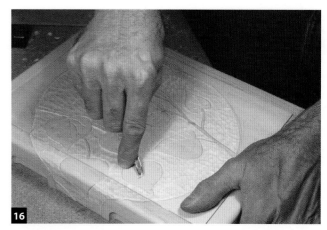

16

Use other chisels to give detail to the carving. Here I use a V-groove gouge to add veins in a leaf.

15

Use the straight chisel to outline the design elements and then the gouge to define the space between.

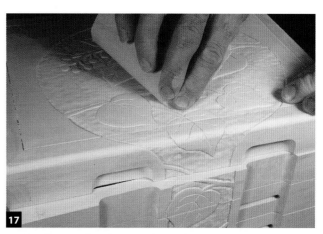

17

Hand sanding completes the carving by gently rounding sharp edges and smoothing the background.

so a trip to the library may be useful. Use a small straight chisel to cut the outline of the carving. Most of my carving is done with a straight chisel and a very shallow gouge that I use to carve away the background areas.

Continue the design on the lid of the box, beginning at the box front, rounding up over the front edge and into the top panel. Use the same leaf shapes and sketched branches. I added the linden berries to conform to the line drawing shown in "Trees of Arkansas" and to add interest to the design. Sand the background with a range of grits moving from coarse to fine. The sanding will soften some of the crisp edges.

I use handheld sandpaper rather than a power sander, which would quickly remove essential details.

## Make the Drawers

Use the same mortise-and-tenon technique as was used in making the inlaid walnut ring box to fit the drawer sides to the drawer fronts and backs. With a 3/16" straight-cut bit, rout the mortises into the drawer fronts, then adjust the fence position and rout the mortises in the box sides.

Use a 1" straight-cut router bit to form the tenons on the drawer sides and backs. Use a 1/8" straight-cut bit to rout for the drawer bottoms to fit. Then with a 3/16" straight-cut bit in the router table,

**18**

A relief cut made on the table saw eases the cut in forming the tenons. The safety blocking has been removed to show the process more clearly.

**19**

Check the fit of the drawer guides before the drawers are assembled. I rout test pieces and check the fit before routing the guide channels in the drawer sides.

**20**

Shape the front edge of the base to reflect the front of the chest by using the router table and straight-cut bit. Remove the waste first with the band saw.

rout the drawer sides to fit the hardwood drawer guides in the box.

Before routing the drawer sides, place the drawer guides in position in the box sides. Carefully measure and cut test pieces to check the fit of the drawer sides before actually routing the channels.

Cut the drawer bottoms to size, then sand all the inside surfaces of the drawer parts. Assemble the drawers, using glue spread in the mortises (make sure you check for square).

Then rout the drawer fronts for the drawer pulls to fit.

Use the router table to rout the front of the base to reflect the shape of the box front. I used a ¾"-radius straight-cut router bit in the router table along with the fence and stop-blocks to position the cut. The parts of the base are assembled using the same technique used in making the base for the triangle tower.

I chose to use very simple pulls modeled after the divider used in the men's jewelry box. They're simple pieces of maple, with the ends rounded on the router table and the top edges slightly rounded with sandpaper.

Use the techniques shown in earlier chapters to make the sliding tray and dividers for the top and drawers. Use quadrant hinges to attach the lid.

**21**

Assemble the parts of the base around the birch plywood panel. The birch plywood serves as both the bottom of the chest and as the spline holding the parts of the base together.

**22**

Make the template for installing the hinges by using the router table and fence with stop-blocks to control the cut. Make two identical pieces. One will be used to make the guide for the left hinge and the other for the right. Additional templates will be needed to rout clearance for the integral lid stops.

**23**

Rout for the left and right hinges to fit. I always do a test piece first to make sure the depth is correct. I use a ¼" router bit and ⁷⁄₁₆" guide bushing in a ½" wide template to cut the space required for a ⁵⁄₁₆" wide hinge.

**24**

Next, rout the clearance required for the stop arms with the plunge router and ⅛" bit. Each side should be routed to just more than half the length of the stop arm.

There are ready-made jigs to assist in installing these hinges, but I chose to make my own. I started with a piece of ¼" Baltic birch plywood and used a ½" straight-cut bit in the router table with stop-blocks to control the position of the cut. Because quadrant hinges require matching left- and right-hand sides, you'll need separate matching jigs to rout for the support arms to fit.

After nailing parts to the jig to allow it to be clamped in place, use the jig to rout in the box corners for the hinges to fit. This technique requires a ¼"

straight cut router bit and a ⁷⁄₁₆" guide bushing. Finally, use screws to attach the base to the carcass after the box is finished and oiled.

# CHAPTER TWENTY-FIVE

# RELIQUARY OF WOOD

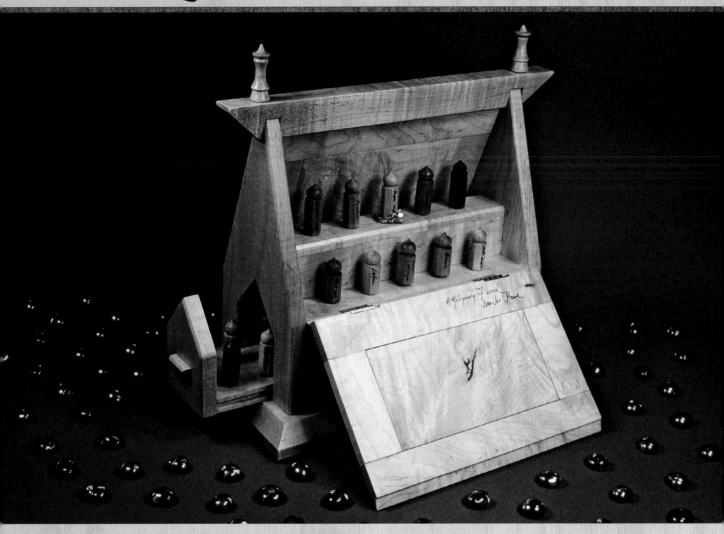

I like to look for inspiration outside the woodworking realm. One of my favorite places in the world is the Nelson-Atkins Museum of Art in Kansas City, Missouri, as it has a great collection of Chinese furniture. My wife and daughter went there with me to celebrate my 50th birthday. At the time, I had also been invited to make a "shrine" for inclusion in an exhibit with other craft artists. In a museum case I discovered a small tin box, beautifully painted, simple, elegant and made to hold precious religious relics. That reliquary is the inspiration for this box, which is made to hold turned and labeled samples of Arkansas hardwoods. It can also be used to hold and display rings.

# MATERIALS LIST

| | | |
|---|---|---|
| Ends | 2 | ½" x 4½" x 8⅜" |
| Sides | 2 | ⅜" x 2⅞" x 9" Includes ¼" tenons |
| Interior parts | 1 | 5⁄16" x 1⅜" x 8¾" |
| Interior parts | 2 | 5⁄16" x 1¼" x 8¾" |
| Interior parts | 2 | ¼" x 1⅜" x 8½" |
| Drawer guides | 2 | ½" x 1¼" x 8¾" |
| Ridge | 1 | 13⁄16" x 1 1⁄16" x 12" |
| Doors | 2 | |
| Horizontal rails | 4 | ⅜" x 1¼" x 8 7⁄16" |
| Stiles | 4 | ⅜" x 1¼" x 4" Includes ½" tenons |
| Panels | 2 | ⅜" x 3 5⁄32" x 6 7⁄32" Includes ⅛" tongues on panel edges |

### *Drawer*

| | | |
|---|---|---|
| Facings | 2 | ½" x 2⅜" x 3 5⁄16" |
| Bottom | 2 | ½" x 2⅜" x 4½" Includes ¼" tenon to fit drawer front |
| Base | 1 | ⅞" x 6" x 11⅛" |

### *Hardware*

| | | |
|---|---|---|
| Brass hinges | 2 pr. | 1" x ⅞" (open width) |
| Exterior turnings | 2 | |
| Hardwood samples | 25 | Turned from octagonal stock |

## Making the Reliquary

The reliquary is made of sugar maple and uses a mortise-and-tenon technique as used in making the inlaid walnut ring box. It's made to hold 15 wood samples or rings in the upper section and an additional 10 in the drawers that open at each end. To prevent warping, the lids are made with floating panels in a frame held together with mortise-and-tenon joints.

This is a more complicated box, but it uses many of the techniques covered in earlier projects. Rather than cover the making of the entire box, this is an overview of some of the more unusual elements of the process.

I resawed the lumber for the end pieces from 5/4 sugar maple. It is important to note that where parts of differing thicknesses are required, resawing need not be at the center of the stock. Resaw the material on the band saw and, using the thickness planer, bring the stock to the desired thicknesses. I made my box ends from ½" stock, the box sides and doors from ⅜" stock and the interior parts from 5⁄16" and 3⁄16" stock.

Saddle joint

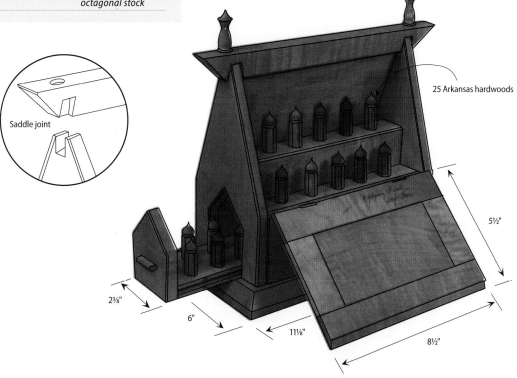

25 Arkansas hardwoods

5½"

2⅜"

6"

11⅛"

8½"

To make efficient use of materials, use the table saw and band saw to make cuts separating the box ends. The point of one end protrudes into the drawer opening of the matching end.

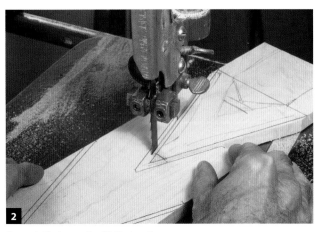

Separate the box ends with the band saw.

Use the sled on the table saw with stop-blocks tacked in place to cut the angled rooflines.

## Make the Ends

To save material, cut the parts out so that the point of one box end enters the drawer space of the next. Make preliminary cuts on the band saw to isolate the ends from each other. Then use the sled on the table saw to trim the ends to final size. At the same time, cut a template piece that can be used for routing the inside of the drawer opening and to check the positions of the mortises as they are made. Define the interior shape of the template piece by making cuts with the table saw and the band saw, and finally shaping with a straight chisel and rasp.

Use the template-following bit to rout the doorway shapes in the end pieces. First, cut away waste with the band saw to ease the router's work and to prevent tear-out. Use a straight chisel to finish the point of the doorway where the template bit was unable to cut. Then rout the mortises in the end pieces for the sides, internal shelves and drawer guides to fit with a ⅛" router bit, fence and stop-blocks on the router table to control the position and length of cut. Rout the mortises to a depth of ¼" for the sides to fit. The mortises for the internal parts should be deep.

Cut the saddle joints into the top of the ends. This joint is for the top crossbeam to fit. Use the band saw and fence to cut into the top, turning it over to make the opposite cut. I clamped a stop-block on the band saw table to control the depth of the cut. Then using a straight chisel, remove the stock between the cuts to finish the joint.

Cut the matching saddle joints in the top beam and then cut it to shape using the table saw and router. To cut the saddle joint, begin with the router table and use a chisel to finish the joint.

## Make the Doors

Mortise and tenon the parts for the doors. Use the router table to rout the mortises following the same steps as used in making the internal parts for the lid for the cherry jewelry chest.

Tenon the side stretchers for the doors using the sled on the table saw or a tenoning jig. Assemble the door parts and, using the chamfering router bit, rout the inside space within the door frame. Then use a sharp chisel to finish the corners. Take the door frames apart and rout the dados for the panels to fit.

Make the door panels following the same technique used for making the wedding ring music box. Use a pilot-

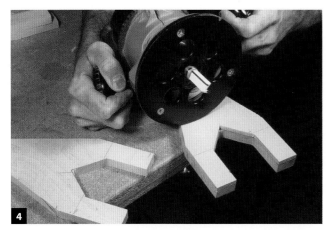

Use a template-following router bit to shape the interior space of the drawers. Use a band saw to cut the rough shape before routing.

Use the router table, fence, stop-blocks and a ⅛" straight-cut bit to form the mortises for the sides and interior parts to fit.

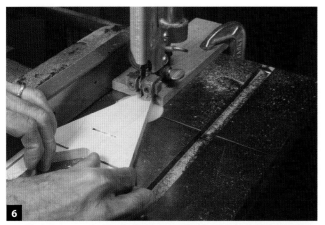

Use the band saw to form the saddle joint for the top beam. A stop-block clamped to the table controls the depth of cut. The fence controls the width of the opening.

Use a chisel to finish the cut.

Use a chisel to finish cutting the saddle joint in the top beam.

Use the mortise-and-tenon techniques on the router table and table saw to form the door frames. Then after chamfering the inside edges of the frames, finish the chamfer into the corners with a chisel.

Make a template from scrap stock and use it with a template-following router bit to shape the drawer ends.

Squeeze glue into the mortises in the ends as the reliquary is assembled. It is amazing how many complicated parts are required for a simple design. Careful fitting of parts allows it to go together easily.

less V-groove bit to chamfer the edges of the panels. Sand the interior edges and routed chamfers on the door parts and panels. After putting glue in the mortises, assemble the doors. Clamp the parts while the glue dries.

## Make the Sides and Interior Parts
Tenon the sides and internal parts following the same steps as used in some of the earlier boxes. Cut the angles on the interior parts and box sides. Cut matching angles on the assembled doors to fit the sides and top beam.

Cut dados on the top shelf for the interior panels to fit. Then cut a tongue on the interior panels sized to fit the dados and cut them to fit between the interior shelves.

## Making the Drawers
Cut some maple stock to the required shape. It should be undersized to allow movement in opening and closing. Rout the mortise in the drawer front for the drawer bottom to fit. Tenon the end of the drawer bottom to fit the mortise. Finally, cut drawer guide slots in the drawer sides.

## Prepare for Assembly
Mark the locations on the interior shelves and drawer bottoms for the wood sample pins to fit. Using a ⅜" bit in the drill press, drill holes about ¼" deep.

Rout the sides and doors for the hinges to fit. Use the router table and a 1" straight-cut bit to cut the hinge mortises. The height of cut should be just less than half of the closed thickness of the hinge.

Rout each of the box parts with a slight chamfer, and sand them through a range of grits from coarse to extra fine. Then do the final shaping of the ridge beam and drill it for the turned finials to fit.

## Turn the Finials and Posts
Use the four jaw-pin chuck on the lathe to turn the finials and interior posts from ½" square stock. Leave most of the posts flat to allow the names of the woods to be inscribed. I use a ⅜" open-end wrench to check the accuracy of the turned tenons for fitting into the holes in the interior shelves. Turn the finials for the top from sugar maple. I chose sugar maple for the finials to leave the brightly colored assortment of woods on the inside a surprise when the reliquary is opened.

Assemble the reliquary and use Danish oil finish to bring out the natural colors of the woods.

## Conclusion
I've met many other woodworkers who when examining my boxes have said, "I just don't have the patience for that sort of work."

Making boxes is a process. Select from the boxes offered in this book to begin your box making adventure, or use the techniques shown here to make boxes of your own design. Feel free to experiment.

It is funny how we will wait patiently at a red light, secure in the knowledge it will turn green. Making boxes is the same thing, except that it is best not to wait. Begin! Proceed! Join the ranks of we who have tried, failed and learned. At some point you will look back to find your own story told in wood.

# WOODWORKING & CREATIVITY

## CERTAINTY & RISK

In his book, "The Nature and Art of Workmanship," David Pye discussed what he viewed as two types of workmanship: that of certainty and that of risk. Tasks like those performed in modern manufacturing, where probabilities of success are high enough to be considered without risk of failure, he describes as being workmanship of certainty. Workmanship like cutting dovetails by hand where a slip of the chisel might mean failure involves workmanship of risk. The task of becoming a "better" woodworker is addressed by attempting to increase the certainties of one's work, either by changing the technology involved or by developing the level of skill of the woodworker. These are choices that woodworkers make every day in selecting our tools and processes. Our culture places so much emphasis on the products that come from woodworking, measuring them against the standards of the manufacturing industries, and tending to overlook that which is essential in their nature – that they are evidence of a process of personal growth and discovery. From my view, it is that process that is ultimately of greatest value. Many times, as I have shown my work in craft fairs, beginning woodworkers have come up to me, and while admiring my work, have been apologetic for their own. But woodworking, at its best, is not finished work. For me, the best projects have not necessarily been the ones that have come out the best. My best projects have been those that have challenged and inspired me to explore new areas in my work, to learn new skills and to transcend what I had thought were my limits. On this scale of measurement, the best workmanship must involve risk. All good design has been achieved through individual and collective effort of trial and error, meaning, of course, that it has evolved through continuing attempts to rectify and learn from the mistakes of the past. Workmanship, whether that of certainty or risk, has evolved through the process of trial and error as well. Unless a person is ready to risk failure, there is no point in beginning. I encourage you to make your very own mistakes without personal recrimination. I am a believer in the principle that crisis and opportunity are the same thing. When I make mistakes-and as a forty-hour-a-week professional, I make many (some of them large) – I have learned to look and listen for the opportunity presented to me to learn something, to improve my work or to practice forgiveness of myself, and occasionally the mistakes I make become the inspiration for new work. Because I work with wood for a living, and because my work must be produced and sold at a price people can reasonably afford. I have become dependent on the use of power tools for many of the operations involved in its production. This is not a bad thing. But the sound of a plane whispering in the ear is a far more engaging and satisfying sound than a router, and I hope that, as the meaning of craftsmanship becomes better understood for its cultural value, new opportunities will emerge for people to enjoy the quieter forms of the woodworking art.

Thorncrown Chapel. Photo by Whit Slemmons.

## CREATIVITY

While it has been said that there is nothing new under the sun, we do witness occasional rearrangements. These rearrangements of the blue for those observing from outside the creative process. For example, here in Eureka Springs we have a small roadside chapel built on a wooded hillside, called Thorncrown Chapel. It was designed by an Arkansas architect, E. Faye Jones, and has received many of the most prestigious architectural awards, including the AIA Gold Medal. To reach Thorncrown Chapel, you must get out of your car and follow a pathway through the woods past limestone outcroppings, and between slender oaks and pines. The chapel's structure, stained only a shade lighter than the bark of the surrounding trees, lift the walls of glass nearly to the height of the trees' towering canopy.

Every element is familiar, and yet the way the elements are put together is new and inspirational. In looking at Thorncrown Chapel from outside the context of E. Faye Jones's career as an architect, the sources of design are nearly incomprehensible. But as I became aware of the other buildings designed by Mr. Jones, I began to see a pattern in the use of elements of design leading to the creation of Thorncrown Chapel. It is clear that Thorncrown Chapel is a high point in a creative process.

If you study the careers of other artists, you find creative process – movement leading from finished work to finished work, each building upon or expanding themes and concepts expressed in earlier work. We woodworkers may think of ourselves as making things, rather than observing ourselves as part of a creative process. To become creative involves a shift from thinking about objects and products to the more subjective reality of process. One of the factors that has enabled me to do quality work has been a focus directed beyond immediate projects toward long-term growth as a woodworker. I look at projects as opportunities for building necessary technical and design skills, as well as an opportunities to express my innermost values. I like to discuss with my customers the merits of various joinery techniques and direct the design of a project toward giving me the opportunity to learn what most interests me. This process not only gives me the growth opportunities I look for, but gives the customer a conscious role in my growth as a craftsman and more involvement in the creative process.

In starting the creative process, the artist or crafts man asks the question, "what is most important to me?", and then begins a search directed toward expressing his or her essential values. It is a process of learning and growth that leads us consciously within, to deeper levels of understanding of ourselves and our relation ship to the outside world.

## RELATIONSHIPS

The drawing on page 183 shows a complex set of relationships within which each of us as a woodworker is unique. We approach our work from a particular focus or set of values. While one of us may be very focused on his tools and the enjoyment he derives from hav-

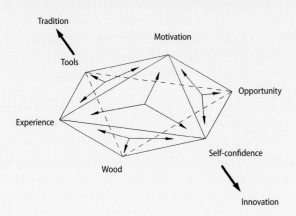

ing and using them, another woodworker may be more interested in the materials he uses; still another may be thinking of a small business to supplement his income, or of finding a way of having nice things in the home without having to pay so much for them, and the pride of accomplishment. I am not implying that any particular focus is correct. I believe that we can become better woodworkers by becoming better acquainted with ourselves as woodworkers, knowing our own values enough to establish a more confident direction in our work, and to thereby express more of our own natures in the work we do with wood. We also differ in levels of motivation, self-confidence and experience. Opportunity is my way of describing the encouragement we receive from our environment to do our work. For an amateur, this encouragement may be a spouse or grand children with a long list of desires, encouraging our time in the shop and allowing our purchase of the tools and materials necessary for our work. It might take the form of being given the opportunity to work with a particularly rare and beautiful piece of wood, or of finding and falling in love with an ancient band saw, or being given an old plane. For the professional, opportunity could take the form of a market for one's work, providing enough economic return and encouragement to continue. Each woodworker also finds himself or herself in a relationship between tradition and innovation. Tradition is the relationship with other woodworkers, past or present, the way things are done or were done. Innovation is

the relationship with the unknown and vast uncharted world of possibilities. It is ironic that today, with the widespread use of the router to do every conceivable woodworking operation, it has become innovative to learn what was traditional in woodworking, the use of hand planes and other non-electrical woodworking tools. It is in the balance between tradition and innovation that real creativity takes place. True creativity is not the result of trying to be different, but of allowing one's own unique values within the complex matrix of relationships to be expressed in one's work. It might come from a woodworker's special relationship with a species of wood, or a particular method of work or with a favorite tool. It can center around one's special loving relationship for a spouse or partner, or around a personal interest outside the shop – fly-fishing perhaps. These connections empower our work and give it greater meaning. Woodworking is not something that takes place only in the isolation of our garages and workshops. It is an expression of the complex relation ships with the worlds of nature, technology, fellow woodworkers, our friends and family, and even with the growth and discovery of ourselves.

## WOOD

Have you ever been to a hardwood lumber dealer and tried to find several matching boards for a project? I wondered why this was such a hard task until I watched the process of grading and sorting lumber at a large mill. A forklift truck dumps up to a thousand board feet of oak at a time into a mechanical bin, which jiggles and shuffles boards to feed them, one at a time, onto a large conveyor. The conveyor then carries them past the trained eyes of the lumber grader, who sorts them by pulling boards into different piles. By the time one board makes it onto the conveyor, its nearest neighbors from the tree are long gone and far away. This is quite a different concept from the photos you may have seen of hardwood logs being sawn, stickered and placed back in the original order just as they were cut from the tree.

I've learned that the very best wood is the wood you've gotten yourself. For me, this means keeping my eyes on the forests and neighborhoods in my community, accepting gifts of trees when they are offered and planting new trees in thanks and appreciation. People have deep feelings for the trees in their yards and in most cases would prefer that a craftsman make use of them rather than have them go into the fireplace or dump. I have a friend, Bob, who has a portable sawmill and will cut logs into lumber for an hourly rate. I can keep and dry lumber in the order that it was cut, which has greater significance to me because it comes from my community and was a gift from friends. I can make sure that there is more of it coming and I can protect it for future generations.

If I were new to woodworking, I'd make friends with someone with one of these saws. I'd call one of the manufacturers and say, "I'm interested in one of your saws. Have you sold one to someone in my town? Where could I see one at work?" Chances are, you'll find someone just like my friend Bob. Of course, the drawback to this approach is that it takes so long. You have to air-dry wood outdoors for several months under cover, then move it indoors for about a year per inch of thickness. Heated and air-conditioned space is best.

Ideals are often complicated. They take time and effort. But it is good to have an objective in mind. In the meantime, I have found that often the most expensive woods are not the most beautiful, and that the characteristics which may make a board unsuitable for some uses, and therefore less costly, may make it more desirable to someone like myself.

## OUR GLOBAL FOREST

As I began my woodworking career, my community of Eureka Springs, Arkansas, was undergoing rapid growth, and I watched as many acres of hardwood and pine forests were bulldozed for new gas stations and motels, and thousands of acres more in the surrounding area were bulldozed to create pastures for livestock. In many cases the trees were not harvested, but simply pushed into ravines or into a pile and burned. During this time as well, it was U.S. Forest Service policy in Arkansas to spray large tracts of hardwoods with defoliants to kill them and allow the faster-growing pines to take over. It became obvious to me that the woods which brought such excitement and wonder to my life were seen as having little value in our culture. It became my hope that by using our hardwoods in a way that informed others of their value, I might become

part of a dialogue leading to their being cherished in our society. We live in a single global forest. The wood thrush that sings in the forest around my home in the summer has a winter life in tropical forests far beyond our national boundary. A woodworker friend shares the following story. He is a wood carver who, despite years of using exotic tropical woods in his work and having a strong fascination with their beauty, had become very concerned about the environmental issues surrounding their use. One day he and his wife were outside his workshop discussing his interest in changing his work to use domestic wood exclusively. She believed that the sale of his work would suffer. He was hoping to find the courage to make the change. And while they talked, a ruby throated hummingbird swooped down and struck him right in the chest. It was an omen that my friend would not ignore. I urge those who work with wood to also work with trees and forests. Whether we choose to use domestic or tropical woods, we have a responsibility to our global forest. When the wood thrush sings in my ten acre wood, I rejoice that somewhere on another continent she still has a home in winter. Some of the ways we can support our global forest are: Plant trees, buy land and protect it from development, join and support organizations like Global Releaf, the World Wildlife Federation and The Nature Conservancy. Use care in cutting, avoid waste, reuse or compost your sawdust. Make beautiful, well-crafted things that future generations will cherish.

## TOOLS

My first tool was an old used Shop Smith that my father gave me as a birthday present in 1962. My Shop Smith and I are both 1948 vintage. The nearly half-century old tool works better now than it did when I first got it – I suspect that my years of almost daily use have finally broken it in. Like most woodworkers that have been doing it for some time, I have gradually accumulated a shop full of tools and have the dilemma of having a difficult time finding space whenever I add anything new. So I am very careful in making decisions about buying tools. Actually, some of the best tools for me have been the ones I've figured out how to do without.

There is a Zen saying that "poverty is your greatest treasure, never trade it for an easy life." There is a very strong temptation to fill our shops with wonderful gadgets that take the risk and opportunities for failure and growth out of our lives. One unfortunate factor in all this is that every tool leaves its mark, and with a world full of woodworker, all using the newest and latest, our work can all start to look alike. From the hand chisel to the computerized milling machine, each tool gives its signature to the finished piece – apparent either in the finished surfaces or in the design accommodations made to allow its use.

I have been learning to be very careful about acquiring tools. At one time, I learned to do without the newest and latest tools because I couldn't afford them. I have since learned that the uniqueness of what I do is there in part because I've figured out my own ways to do my work. And while I doubt that the techniques I work with are unique, I get some personal satisfaction from having discovered them for myself.

It takes a great deal of time to exhaust the possible uses of any given tool, and it takes time and practice to develop a skilled relationship with it. Having too much to relate to by having too many tools in the shop can deprive a beginner of the opportunity to develop meaningful relationships with any of your tool. You can find yourself locked up in indecision over whether to use this tool or that one, when either would do the job.

## THE JOY OF DOING WITHOUT
We, as woodworkers, are frequently fooled into believing chat some whatsit is needed, when perhaps our souls crave the experience of learning to do without. We live in a highly technological age, but many of us are called toward a simpler relationship with wood, using hand tools wherever possible and finding greater pleasure and satisfaction in the process of work than in the accomplishment of finished products. It is easy to be led by television woodworking or even by the pages of a book such as this to think that certain equipment will be necessary to do woodworking, and yet many woodworkers make a conscious effort to rely on their personal inventiveness and take great pleasure in sustaining traditional techniques.

As a professional woodworker; I've always been so close on the cash flow that I seldom have the money to buy new tools. So I make do with what I have and

reap the benefit of discovering my own inventiveness and creativity. My favorite tools are actually the oldest ones in my shop. They are like very old friends. That old song line, "Make new friends, but keep the old; one is silver and the other gold," is as true of our tools as of the people in our lives.

I try to keep a balance in my work between the pleasure I derive from it and the efficiency necessary to survive as a professional. This balance is something that all of us face as woodworkers. We may have slightly impatient spouses who wonder what's taking so long in the shop. We may be having to justify in our own minds the expense of tools and materials when we perhaps started out with the delusions of saving money while furnishing our homes.

I think the answer to much of this is to savor the moment – realize there is a balance to be sought some-

where between the fully equipped shop and the some-thing-from-nothing approach. The point of balance is unique for each of us. We need not respond like robots to the latest tool or technique. Cherish the inefficiencies of the old and the history it holds dear. Find satisfaction and pleasure in doing without and find new and wonderful levels of inventiveness, creativity and satisfaction in our woodworking lives.

## ATTENTION & MEDITATION

Woodworking can be a dangerous occupation or hobby. The high level of attention it requires precludes working when angry or preoccupied with outside-the-shop matters. I learned this the hard way, by dadoing my thumb while finishing a small project the day before getting married. It is important to me that my shop be a place of peace, allowing me to focus my attention directly on the task at hand. I've found this to be the only safe way to work, and infinitely rewarding. I believe the

thing that engages so many people in woodworking is what meditation teachers call mindfulness. Many of us have entered a timeless space in our workshops and in our work, in which we have been so engaged by the processes of making things that we take no note of time passing, and are at last awakened to external consciousness by the words, "Aren't you coming to bed?" Even after 20 years, woodworking can do that to me. For beginning woodworkers, the excitement of learning new things empowers our ability to focus undisturbed attention on processes happening at our fingertips. By pursuing the development of new skills and practicing new techniques, by developing new designs, and acquiring new tools and learning their use, we gain the energy required to focus our attention and our enthusiasm. In addition, the ability to focus your attention grows through regular practice like every other human activity. I have come to believe, through watching the various relationships involved in my woodworking activities, that there is actually a lot more going on than

meets the eye, that would be described as coincidental or spiritual, depending on your particular perspective. An artist friend of mine, Louis Freund, explains that the artist's work is essentially spiritual in nature, as we create work that has never been seen before, risking censorship and failure while guided by our own inner vision. For me, meditation is a way to integrate all the complex relationships of woodworking into a single vision. I practice two forms of meditation: one that could be called sitting meditation, and a second, active meditation, the practice of dual awareness. Sitting meditation is a way to gain composure and focus. I find it very useful to sit in a comfortable position for a few minutes each day. I meditate to get clear and focused on who I am and what I'm doing, keeping in mind that I may not be here to change the world, and that my working with wood may as well be the way in which I myself am changed. In practicing dual awareness, I simply proceed with the task at hand, but with my attention divided between a focus on inner purpose and on what my hands are doing. It is good to begin practicing this on some of the less dangerous jobs in the shop. After a while it becomes an almost automatic way of working. As you practice this meditation, you may begin to actually sense the downward response in energy flow that comes from contact with inner purpose. For me, part of the challenge of being a woodworker is maintaining a connection to higher purpose. I am personally not satisfied with making stuff. The world is already full of meaningless things that satisfy some immediate needs but are quickly hustled off to landfills. I have hopes that my work can awaken, and inform, while expressing caring and concern for our natural world. We work within the context of a tradition going back thousands of years to the first mortise-and-tenon joint. We work with woods grown in forests that are thousands of years old. We work in a time of human history when basic human values seem confused, and when our unreasoned misuse of the Earth's resources must be questioned. Meditation helps me to reconcile these factors and move toward what I believe to be good works. Human beings are unique among the inhabitants of our planet in that we have choices in our sense of self. It is like television in that we can identify with a variety of self-images in the same way one can watch a variety of channels. We can perceive of ourselves as purely physical beings concerned with fulfilling physical needs; emotional beings concerned with pleasing other people to gain emotional support and acknowledgement; mental beings wrestling with intellectual concepts; or spiritual beings connected with others through these means and more. A normal human being is continually shifting focus or channel surfing throughout the clay. Meditation is a means by which I can make an effort to observe myself and begin reconciling all the various aspects of being human.

While for some, the woodworking shop may be a retreat from the concerns of the world and a place to recharge the spirit before reentering the workplace, mine has become a place through which I connect with the world, try to learn from it, and hopefully reconnect with and share human values that appear in some ways to be endangered.

## ON THE MEANING OF RECREATION

I subscribe to the rec.woodworking news group on the Internet. It gives me the opportunity to communicate with other woodworkers, share some of what I have learned, and learn from their experience and enthusiasm. It is a group of mainly amateur woodworkers. The rec in the title refers to recreation, bur even a professional wood worker like me can find kindred spirits there. To recreate means to restore, refresh, create anew, to put fresh life into; refresh or restore in body or mind, especially after work, by some form of play, amusement or relaxation. Recreation is more than just having some thing to do after work. The time we spend daydreaming, planning, browsing through the latest catalogs, hanging out in the news group and working in the shop is time for renewal and restoration of spirit. Whether our hard work creates something to show is beside the point. The hidden object of our pursuit is the re-creation of ourselves.

A friend of mine, Joe, is married to an outspoken and vivacious woman who grew up in a family with very sophisticated tastes. When he completed his first and only attempt at woodworking, an entertainment center made from pine, it didn't come close to resembling anything that Babs would call furniture. You can imagine the scene: Joe basking in the delight of accomplishment and Babs, not being one to miss the opportunity to say what's on her mind, lets it rip. Joe's foray in to the world of recreational woodworking ground to a screeching halt. This happened several years ago. The entertainment center was cut into kindling and went up in smoke along with the last of Joe's woodworking aspirations. There is still a touch of pain in his voice when he describes his only woodworking adventure.

There are two woodworkings, the first being the idealized one, the woodworking of expectations, where everything turns out perfect. The spouse is pleased, each and every joint is of Krenovian perfection, and we are exalted on the shoulders of our peers. Then there is the real thing, the nitty gritty. It consists of wood putty, not enough clamps, the desperate need for a lumber stretcher, and all the questions asked in the news group when the confidence of "Yes! I can do that!" meets the reality of "Oops!"

So I try to keep things in perspective: We are all newbies at something. Our encouragement of each other is essential. The best woodworking experiences are the ones that bring us humility, understanding and personal growth. Our best work comes from our willingness to take chances and risk failure. Perfection exists only as an objective to be reached toward. And moment-by-moment satisfaction from the process of woodworking is the best reward. So, have fun! Join an online forum like rec.woodworking! Share what you've learned with others! If you find Joe out there in the world, invite him to your shop and get him started with something smaller than an entertainment center. How about a box?

## INTENTIONAL IMPERFECTION

Many cultures around the world share an interesting notion of perfection. Amish quilt makers would leave a single stitch undone rather than make the "perfect" quilt, expressing their belief that only God could make something perfect. Among weavers in Turkey, the same idea is found. Many Chinese and Japanese artists believe that their work should include "incompleteness and imperfection," an emptiness that leaves room for further growth.

I've never had much problem with perfection. I've yet to make the perfect box or the perfect piece of furniture. I can't imagine in my own work the need to leave

something imperfect as a statement, to ever complete the perfect piece and find myself in that predicament. A craftsman sees the points where his or her own work needs refinement – the little slips of the saw or chisel, the sanding marks, the slight rounding where something should be straight. Fortunately, most observers don't notice these things and accept our work, seeing it as perfect despite its many flaws or, at least, choosing to pay attention to its strengths.

In woodworking, we face the inevitable. As human beings and not machines, we make mistakes in measuring. Things slip both from the fingers and from the mind as we work. Wood is not the perfect material. It has imperfections. It is always expanding and contracting in response to changes in climate, challenging the artist in his efforts to make the perfect piece.

A gentleman I once met is friends with the famous rocking chair maker; Sam Maloof. The gentleman told me the following story. Sam was visiting Japan and was shown a beautiful storage box for sweaters. He noted how precisely it was made and marveled to his hosts that something could be made of real wood to such close tolerances. He asked, "Doesn't this lid swell shut in the humid summer months?" His hosts answered, "Yes, but it is a sweater box. Who would open it then?"

As we develop our skills through new projects, our ideas about perfection evolve. Perfection is elusive, always just beyond our reach like the carrot on the stick.

I am lucky to live in a community that has encouraged my work with wood. I often go into friends' homes and find work that I had done years ago when my skills were not as well developed. I can look at each piece from a critical perspective, finding fault with my earlier shortcomings, or I can find in each piece some small steps that were taken in my personal growth as a woodworker and feel honored that the work is cherished and loved despite its flaws.

Growth toward perfection is part of the story that woodworking tells. When you begin to understand that woodworking is storytelling, each slip of the chisel becomes part of the perfection of the finished piece. With this in mind, you have no reason not to begin making boxes.

# SOME NOTES ABOUT SAFETY

You will notice that most of the photos in this book were taken with the machines off so that I could pose those photos without putting my hands and fingers at unnecessary risk. A good rule of thumb for keeping your thumbs is to keep your hands and fingers a safe distance from the blade. Push blocks, push sticks, hold-downs and featherboards are designed to do just that. They can be quickly made or you may buy them from your tool supplier. You may be familiar with the common push stick. They keep your hands and fingers a safe distance from the blade but offer little control. Safe woodworking, whichever tool you are using requires control as well as keeping your hands a safe distance from the cutting edge.

I make most of my push blocks from scrap wood, so that I have no hesitation to cut into them when necessary or to throw them away when they have served their purpose in making a carefully controlled cut. In fact, these essential woodworking tools, when used correctly, make your woodworking more accurate and keep you safe. Push blocks are most oven used standing up in a vertical position following the fence, but they are also useful laying flat on the surface of the table saw or router table in conjunction with another push block used in the normal fashion or with a plastic foam backed a paddle shown in the photo top right to hold the stock down, for instance, when making a dado cut.

Even the eraser end of a pencil, when used to hold a small part on the sled, can provide enough control for a safer cut, while keeping the hands the right distance from the blade.

Featherboards and foam or sand paper backed plastic paddles are both useful to guide wood safely through the cut. Featherboards on the table saw should be used on the front side of the cut, and not where the pressure would push the cut-off stock into the blade.

One of my favorite push block designs is shown on page 190. It's pistol like grip provides some leverage for pressing down on the stock as you guide wood through the cut. Other push blocks and hold downs are identified in the captions.

A variety of push blocks, shown clockwise from 12 o'clock: Long push block for ripping or jointing long stock, pistol grip push block, foam backed plastic paddle, a fresh pencil with good eraser, and a custom designed wood hold down.

A variety of featherboard configurations, shown clockwise from top: Featherboards may be held in place with strong magnets or lock in the miter gauge slots in the top of the saw. They may also be quickly made from wood, be clamped in place and be discarded when they're worn.

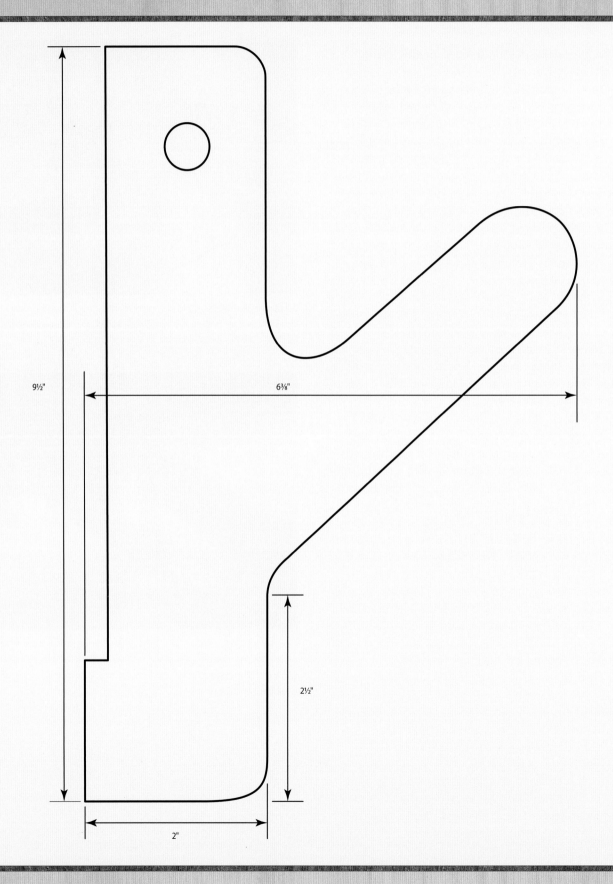

9½"

6⅜"

2½"

2"

Distributed in Canada by Fraser Direct
100 Armstrong Avenue
Georgetown, Ontario L7G 5S4
Canada

Distributed in the U.K. and Europe by
F+W Media International, LTD
Pynes Hill Court
Pynes Hill
Rydon Lane
Exeter
EX2 5SP

Tel: +44 1392 797680

Distributed in Australia by Capricorn Link
P.O. Box 704
Windsor, NSW 2756
Australia

Visit our website at popularwoodworking.com or our consumer website at shopwoodworking.com for more woodworking information.

Other fine Popular Woodworking Books are available from your local bookstore or direct from the publisher.

ISBN-13: 978-1-4403-4165-6

19   18   17   16      5   4   3   2   1

Editor: *Scott Francis*
Designers: *Daniel Pessell & Angela Wilcox*
Production Coordinator: *Debbie Thomas*

# Read This Important Safety Notice

## METRIC CONVERSION CHART

| | | |
|---|---|---|
| Inches | Centimeters | 2.54 |
| Centimeters | Inches | 0.4 |
| Feet | Centimeters | 30.5 |
| Centimeters | Feet | 0.03 |
| Yards | Meters | 0.9 |
| Meters | Yards | 1.1 |

a content + ecommerce company

# Ideas ▪ Instruction ▪ Inspiration

## Receive FREE downloadable bonus materials when you sign up for our FREE newsletter at popularwoodworking.com.

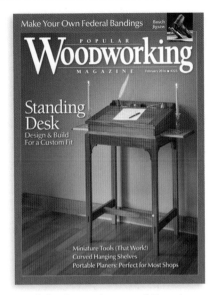

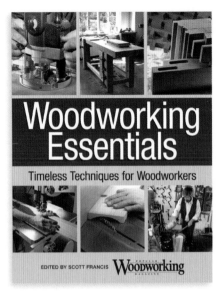

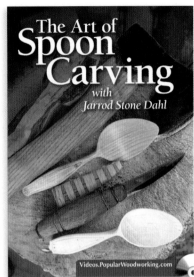

Find the latest issues of *Popular Woodworking Magazine* on newsstands, or visit **popularwoodworking.com**.

These and other great Popular Woodworking products are available at your local bookstore, woodworking store or online supplier. Visit our website at **shopwoodworking.com**.

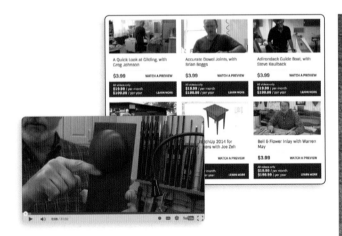

## Popular Woodworking Videos

Subscribe and get immediate access to the web's best woodworking subscription site. You'll find more than 400 hours of woodworking video tutorials and full-length video workshops from world-class instructors on workshops, projects, SketchUp, tools, techniques and more!

**videos.popularwoodworking.com**

## Visit our Website

Find helpful and inspiring articles, videos, blogs, projects and plans at **popularwoodworking.com**.

 For behind the scenes information, become a fan at **Facebook.com/ popularwoodworking**.

 For more tips, clips and articles, follow us at **twitter.com/pweditors**.

 For visual inspiration, follow us at **pinterest.com/popwoodworking**.

 For free videos visit **youtube.com/popwoodworking**.